Vinu Abraham is a well-known writer of short stories, novels, film scripts and essays in Malayalam. He has published twenty-three books, including eleven short story collections and four novels. A winner of several prestigious Malayalam literary awards, he has also won the Best Scriptwriter Award for the film *Parudeesa* in the Mexico International Film Festival. A native of Nedungadappally in Pathanamthitta district of Kerala, he lives in Thiruvananthapuram.

C.S. Venkiteswaran is a reputed film critic and essayist writing in both Malayalam and English.

Arathy Ashok is a professor of English who engages in translations and other writings.

THE LOST HEROINE

Vinu Abraham

Translated from the Malayalam by
C.S. Venkiteswaran and Arathi Ashok

SPEAKING
TIGER

SPEAKING TIGER BOOKS LLP
4381/4, Ansari Road, Daryaganj
New Delhi 110002

This edition published in paperback by Speaking Tiger Books 2020

ISBN: 978-93-89958-40-9
eISBN:978-93-89958-41-6

10 9 8 7 6 5 4 3 2 1

Typeset in Garamond Premier Pro by SÜRYA, New Delhi
Printed at Chaman Enterprises, New Delhi

To the fond memories of
Baby Thomas, Appa and Amma

'We have kept one of her tears, which rolled down to us, in a celluloid box. An odourless, tasteless, colourless tear, a drop from the purest spring.'

—Luis Buñuel in his review of Carl Dreyer's
The Passion of Joan of Arc

INTRODUCTION

I HAVE ALWAYS been passionate about history in its various manifestations, including the history of cinema and literature. But I had never expected that one day I would be drawn into the exploration of a very exciting chapter in Malayalam cinema—the very origin of the film industry in Kerala in the era of silent films. Though Malayalam is my mother tongue, the idea of writing a novel based on my discoveries would have seemed an even wilder proposition to me back then.

It was on a pleasant evening during the International Film Festival of Kerala (IFFK), at the Kairali theatre complex in Trivandrum (now Thiruvanthapuram), that it all began. A group of

Dalit artists led by Baby Thomas, a writer, was holding a protest demonstration and handing out leaflets to onlookers. The upshot of the protest was that all concerned with the history of Malayalam cinema, including the state government, film industry and film historians, have never acknowledged the fact that it was P.K. Rosy, a Dalit girl from Trivandrum, who was the heroine of *Vigathakumaran* (*The Lost Child*), the first film made in Kerala in 1928 and released in 1930. Their contention was that Rosy, who faced a cruel fate on account of her acting, should be accorded proper recognition as the Mother of Malayalam Cinema. The leaflet also contained a short poem commemorating Rosy, penned by noted poet Kureepuzha Sreekumar.

This was a shocking revelation to me. Though I had a vague knowledge about *Vigathakumaran* and its maker, Dr J.C. Daniel, I had never come across the fact that the film's making and its release involved a unique saga, including that of Rosy. In the days that followed, this revelation continued to haunt me. I felt that something, perhaps a feature, should be written about Rosy and the making of the film. Thus, I set about making enquiries regarding it.

Before long, I was guided into the presence of Kunnukuzhi S. Mani, a Dalit historian and writer, and R. Gopalakrishnan, a film historian and still-life photographer. Extensive interactions with both followed and soon I realized that I was on to something which could not be contained in a mere feature piece. Besides this, I was also helped by an article regarding the beginning of Malayalam cinema by the late film historian Chelangattu Gopalakrishnan. Eventually it emerged that if I were to write strictly about only the provable facts regarding the life of Rosy, it would not amount to even three pages.

Even though the broad outlines of Rosy's life could be gleaned, there were lots of gaps in her narrative. In fact, not even a mugshot of her face was available anywhere. Very soon, it dawned on me that I should go for a narrative which would employ liberal doses of imagination, albeit conforming to the broad parameters of her known realities and historical honesty—in fact, a novel. It was thus that I embarked on the journey of this novel.

After about three years of research and intermittent writing, *Nashtanaika* (the Malayalam title of this novel) was published in 2008 by Current Books, a prestigious imprint in Malayalam based in Thrissur. Since then it has seeped into Malayali literary and cultural consciousness in varied forms.

Theatre productions, both amateur and professional, have adapted the novel. A unique audio version of the novel involving nearly twenty artists lending their voices was launched in 2014.

Perhaps the crowning glory of the general acceptance of the novel came when it was adapted as a film by veteran director Kamal. Titled *Celluloid*, the film, starring South Indian heartthrob Prithviraj as J.C. Daniel, with debutante actor Chandini playing Rosy, became a massive box office triumph as well as a critical success. The novel still continues to attract new readers with new editions coming out from Chintha Publishers.

Now a few words about the period of the novel: It was at the time when Regent Sethu Lakshmi Bayi was ruling Travancore state (present-day south Kerala) that the narrative of this novel takes place. British rule in the state was imposed through the British Resident posted in Trivandrum. It was also an era when casteism along with its rules of untouchability between upper-caste Hindus and lower castes was prevailing, though progressive social movements were waging battles against it.

Interestingly, as a creative writer, the short story is my favourite medium and it is in that format that I write frequently. It is my experience that most of my readers too relate to that genre. Yet, *Nashtanaika* has turned out to be a milestone in my writing career. It was as if for more than seventy years this painful saga regarding the origin of Malayalam cinema was waiting to be presented to the world by me. I certainly thank destiny in choosing me for this mission.

Malayalam cinema has come a long way from its humble beginnings and recently celebrated its ninetieth year (based on the making of *Vigathakumaran* in 1928). As such, it is heartening to me that my novel is now reaching a global platform through this English version. Here I offer my sincere gratitude towards the two translators, C.S. Venkiteswaran and Arathy Ashok. I hope that the saga of Rosy and Daniel will find an echo in the hearts of non-Malayali readers too.

VINU ABRAHAM
March 2020

ONE

'ROSY, ARE YOU feeling sleepy?'

Startled, Rosy opened her eyes. Standing in front of her was Daniel. She hurriedly began to get up from the grass mat.

'No need to get up now. We'll call you when it is time for you to act,' he said, and walked away.

How could I tell Daniel Sir that I had not been sleeping but praying? I was praying to God that whatever I do should come out good, and that this cinema business should go well. It is a habit from my childhood—whenever I am doing something important, I start only after prayers.

Today is the day I am going to become a film actress—a heroine in a film! The first film heroine in this land of Malayalam! Only a few minutes left for that...soon, the camera will capture my face and body into film.

A fortnight back, when Johnson came home and told her about this, she couldn't believe it at all.

It was afternoon. Her Amma and Appan had gone out for work. Since she had no work that day, she had stayed at home. Having had her tapioca and fish curry, she was sitting under the papaya tree in the front yard, washing the pots. Then she heard someone clearing his throat. When she raised her head to look, she saw Johnson standing outside the hut. *Hey! How come Johnson Sir is here?*

It was quite unusual. He was from a well-to-do family and lived in a house by the road. He was a handsome young man. Soon after they moved from Amathara and settled here, Rosy had stumbled into him on the road, and he had introduced himself.

He was walking towards her from the other side. When he saw her, he suddenly stopped and asked with a wide smile on his face, 'Koche, your name is Rosy, isn't it?'

She was totally flustered, but said, 'Yes.'

'You are a good artist, isn't it?'

She was at a loss for a moment. She gazed at him curiously.

'I have seen you acting in Kakkarissi plays. It was good. You performed really well in that role which has only been played by men until now.'

She didn't know how to respond. Upon receiving such a compliment, that too from a handsome young man, she could not stop herself from breaking into a smile that lit up her face.

'Okay, see you later.' With that, Johnson walked past.

Later she came to know that Johnson too acted in plays and had a reputation as a good actor. After that, whenever they met on the road, he used to give her a charming smile. She would also smile back shyly.

'Come on. I have come to your house, and you are not inviting me in?' When Johnson Sir said this, Rosy grew nervous. He was right. Confused at his sudden appearance, she had forgotten basic etiquette and was standing blankly staring at him. But in a hut like theirs where could she invite him to sit? There was only a low stool with one wobbling leg.

'Hey, don't worry about me. I will stand here. Are your Amma or Appan here?'

'No. They have gone out for work.'

'Okay. I will tell you why I came. I came here to invite you to an acting programme. When I say acting, it is not Kakkarissi or a play. It is film acting. Cinema.'

Rosy's eyes widened. Cinema? She had only heard about it; she had not seen any cinema so far. She didn't even know what it was.

Johnson explained: 'There is a young man named J.C. Daniel. He is from a rich family, the son of an apothecary. He is going to make a film in Trivandrum, which will be the first film in the land of Malayalam. For that purpose, he has constructed a "studio" in Pattom and has already shot some portions of the film...Now he is about to begin portions where the heroine is to appear.'

Though he had tried in several places, he couldn't find a heroine. As his friend, Johnson too was in search of the heroine. 'Yesterday, suddenly I remembered your face. You have the looks and figure of Sarojini, the heroine of the film, as described to me by Daniel. My mind says: Rosy is the heroine of this film.'

God! What am I hearing? Rosy from a poor Pulaya hut in Thycaud could become a heroine in the magical world of cinema!

She looked around her. No, the world around her was still there. Her hut was still there, beside a string of other small thatched huts. Her dress was still that mundu and blouse, soiled and tattered.

She smiled inwardly.

'Rosy, why are you standing there without saying anything? Don't you like to act?'

He asks me whether I would like to act! It is my life! But...

'Ayyo! Sir, I am really happy that you invited me to act. But there are some problems.'

'What problems?' The smile on Johnson's face faded.

After a moment's hesitation, Rosy opened her heart: Until a year ago, she, her father Paulose and Amma Kunji were staying in Amathara. She was the first woman to perform in a Kakkarissi play. It was the famous Govindan Asan from Amathara who had introduced her to the stage. Initially some male members had arguments with Govindan Asan about giving her a role in the play. But the audience had already begun to like Rosy and were enamoured by her performance, so such opposition gradually fizzled out.

When she became well-known as an actress in Kakkarissi plays, another group of people approached Rosy—drama companies that performed plays in the Tamil style. When one such company came to know that there was a possibility of finding a girl who was ready to act in female roles, they invited her to act in their plays also. She replied she would do so only if Asan agreed to it. Thus she started acting in plays with Asan's permission, and earned repute as a good actress.

But when the next occasion came for her to act in Kakkarissi plays, the Tamil drama company opposed it, saying that it was not possible. They insisted that, from then on, Rosy could act only in their plays. This condition enraged Rosy. She said she was not going to act in their plays any more, and went back to Asan to perform in Kakkarissi plays again.

Following that, the people from the drama company and their rowdies began to haunt Asan's Kakkarissi plays and create disturbances there. One night, while the play was in progress, the hubbub turned into a big ruckus ending in a physical fight. Many people, including Rosy, were hurt in the stone-throwing that ensued.

After that, Paulose and Kunji decided not to send Rosy to act in Kakkarissi plays. Moreover, they also decided to shift residence from Amathara. But there was another reason for moving. Paulose and Kunji had identified a boy who was a relative of Kunji as a bridegroom for Rosy. The boy's parents had also agreed to the proposal. But due to Rosy's tiff with the theatre company and the ruckus that followed, the boy and his family withdrew from that proposal. Paulose and Kunji considered it a disgrace, and decided to move from Amathara to start a new life elsewhere.

Rosy left her acting career behind, and from the day they moved to Thycaud, like her Amma, she too worked at the farms and fields doing wage labour, cutting and selling grass and so on.

Johnson listened to everything and said: 'So, your Appan and Amma won't allow you to act, is it?' He thought for a moment, and then said, 'Let us do one thing. I will come back by dusk when Paulose and Kunji are at home and discuss the matter with them. This is not a low-class affair, but something that involves people with money and class. No harm will come to you. Not only that, a bright future awaits you, Rosy. I will talk to your Appan and convince him.'

From the moment Johnson left, Rosy was simultaneously ruled by feelings of happiness and anxiety. *The cinema is a big affair. And I have had the great fortune to receive an invitation to act in it as a heroine. But will my parents, who are allergic to the very mention of acting, allow me to act? Even if Johnson Sir pleads with them, will they change their minds?*

While doing odd jobs at the hut or sitting idle, Rosy's mind was restless until evening. If Mala were with her, she could have told her everything and thus felt relieved. Mala was Rosy's closest friend and stayed in the hut next to hers. She too had gone for work in the paddy field and would return only by dusk.

Paulose was a helper at the kitchen in the bungalow that belonged to the missionary sayip at LMS church. After finishing his work, he usually returned home only when darkness descended. Every evening, it was Kunji who reached home first.

At first Rosy was hesitant about whether she should tell her all the things that Johnson Sir had said. Amma had never liked her going to act in the Kakkarissi plays. She was of the opinion that girls shouldn't go for such 'jumping-and-leaping' business. When Govindan Asan had come to request them for permission for her to join Kakkarissi, it was given due to Rosy's Appan's magnanimity. He realized how much Rosy yearned to act and so he allowed her to go with Asan.

Later when the trouble with the drama company happened, and it began to affect their lives, Amma gave both of them a severe scolding.

'This song-and-dance is not for us Christians.

Maybe we were converted to Christianity only recently. Still, this old song-and-dance of Pulayas is not for us.' She also didn't forget to mention that all this was a punishment from God for not listening to her. That day didn't she, out of fear of God, warn Appan that he should not allow Rosy to join it?

Anyway, let Johnson Sir himself explain it to them directly. Still, her mind remained jumpy.

The porridge for supper was boiling over the pot kept on the fire, and though Rosy was sitting in front of it, she didn't notice. Seeing this, Kunji shouted at her: 'Penne, what's this? What are you dreaming about?'

Usually Paulose reached his hut as soon as the gas lights in the lamp posts of the city were beginning to be lit. That day, even after the gas lamps had been lit, he was not back in his hut.

And when he did reach, there was something special about it. When he came, Johnson too was with him. Rosy was watching them with wonder. Johnson was saying something to her Appan, who in turn, was laughing loudly.

Standing in the front yard, Johnson noticed the expression of wonder on Rosy's face in the moonlight. 'Koche, your Appan has agreed to everything. I caught him on the way and convinced him.'

Paulose looked at Rosy and smiled.

But there was a bigger hurdle than Appan in front of her, and Rosy wondered how Johnson Sir was going to get over that. *I wonder what all my Amma will say once she gets to know of this!*

When she was informed, Kunji exploded in front of Johnson then and there.

It was followed by a concerted effort at conciliation on the part of Johnson and Paulose. Details about the family status of Johnson, the greatness and high social position of the family of Daniel who was producing the film etcetera poured through their words, and began to influence Kunji.

They convinced Kunji that those behind it were not like the poor people who performed Kakkarissi or those who staged Tamil plays; people of high status and standing from the city were involved in this affair, and no harm would come to Rosy by associating with it. Above all, what ultimately pacified Kunji was their assertion that Rosy would also get a good remuneration for it.

Even then, when Kunji expressed her anxiety about whether it was worthy of Christians like them, Johnson said, with a disarming smile on his face: 'Look, dear sister, think of this. Aren't we two—me and Daniel—Christians too? Wasn't cinema itself discovered by sayips who were also Christians? Cinema is something that is very much ours.'

Rosy was standing in a corner and listening to all the justifications that Johnson Sir elaborated to achieve his objective; when she heard all that, a laugh broke out inside her. *This Johnson Sir is really smart! He is also able to address my parents, who are Pulayas, very liberally by calling them 'Anna' and 'Akka'—brother and sister. Like the upper castes, the Nadar Christians too never treated the Pulayas with respect. Though one listens to the speeches at the church, that all who are Christians are children of God and all that, not a single Nadar considered a Pulaya his equal. And here is Johnson Sir, in a voice brimming with honey and milk, honouring my Appan and Amma! Anyway, he ultimately succeeded in getting what he wanted.*

That night, in the prayers before sleep, Paulose pleaded to God for His mercy as Rosy embarked on this new journey. After the prayers, Paulose told Rosy: 'Me and your Amma are sending you with Johnson Sir now with good intentions. But you should always proceed with the thought of God in your mind. Though we are Amma and Appan to three children, in effect, we only have you now.'

Kunji hugged her to her bosom, and ran her

fingers through her hair. Rosy saw her Amma's eyes brimming with tears.

'Oh, what is all this? It is as if I am going somewhere far away leaving you all! First of all, who knows whether I will be selected for the cinema? Before that, why all this?'

What Paulose said was true. Though they had three children, only Rosy was with them now. It had been like that for the last two years.

There was Thankamma who was elder to Rosy, and Pathrose, her younger brother. Thankamma got married four or five years ago, and was now living in a village called Chavara with her husband Rajappan. Rajappan was working as a permanent labourer for one of the richest farmers in the region. Rajappan and Thankamma rarely came—sometimes once in a year—to visit them.

Even as a child, Pathrose was always prone to various ailments. His life was miserable; his body was very lean with ugly scabs all over his body. It was Rajappan who put forward the proposal after being witness to Pathrose's misery. There was a very good vaidyan—medic—in Chavara, who was very close to Rajappan's employer. If they could get him to treat Pathrose, it might bear fruit.

It was thus that Pathrose was sent to Chavara

with Rajappan and Thankamma when they once came to visit them at Trivandrum. After examining Pathrose, the vaidyan said: 'I will treat and cure him; but it will take time. It may take up to three or four years. As I have to see him frequently for treatment, he should stay in Chavara.'

Initially, Appan and Amma were reluctant to send their only male offspring, however ill he may be, to a faraway place. But Rajappan's good intentions gave both of them great hope, that their son, whose life was being made miserable by illness, would be cured.

Then the relief from the financial burden of meeting the expenses of his treatment, at a time when they themselves were often finding it difficult to make both ends meet. Thus after sending their son far away, they were living here in the hope that one day he would come back fully cured.

Having put off the lights the hut gradually went to sleep, but Rosy lay down thinking of several things and praying repeatedly. *Oh God, let no harm come to my Appan and Amma because of me.*

TWO

ROSY HAD GOT permission from her father and mother to act in the movies, but she needed somebody else's consent and blessing too. *Be it a movie or anything else, if I am going to be an artist, I must get his blessings.*

Govindan Asan. The man who first brought her to the world of art. The Asan who was lord of the world of drama, who had changed her into Kakkalathi or Parvathi Devi, the characters that captivated the minds of the audience. Until then, she was a mere wisp of a girl who had studied up to the third standard and who eked out a living by working in the fields or cutting and selling grass for cattle feed.

Rosy had seen the Kakkarissi drama for the first time at the festival in Amathara's Marutha temple. She had gone to see the play with Neeli Akkan who stayed nearby.

Kakkarissi was not allowed to be performed at the high-caste temples. It was staged only in the low-caste temples where Marutha, Kali, Kuli or Chamundi were enshrined.

The Kakkarissi play usually stretches through the whole night. That time it was performed continuously for three nights by Govindan Asan's group. Though Asan's house and his school, Nataka Kalari, were near Amathara, it was the first time she was seeing him.

All Kakkarissi plays have only one story. But different troupes add speeches, jokes and dialogues as needed, depending on their talent and imagination.

The story is about how Shiva, Parvathi and Ganga came down to earth to subdue the wicked. Once upon a time, the good people on earth suffered because of overpopulation and the unbearable actions of the wicked. Paramashiva came down to the earth in answer to the heartrending prayers of the good people. As the cruel would recognize the gods and thus go into hiding, Narada advised them to travel the earth in disguise. Shiva was disguised as Kakkalan or snake charmer and Parvathi and Ganga as Kakkalathi or Vettuvathi.

Travelling thus, they reached palaces and the houses of the overlords of the bandits and demons. Everywhere they unearthed evil powers and suppressed them. At the end of the play, the demons try to attack Parvathi; she curses them and turns them into owls, cats, lizards. But soon, seeing their sorry plight, the goddess herself gives them deliverance. The demons, on attaining their old forms, pledge that they will not hurt anybody again in the future.

The Kakkarissi play opened before Rosy a new world of experience that she had not known before—an experience called art. She was very much enamoured by the role of Parvathi. Parvathi was a beauty, and Rosy was enthralled by her dance steps, her songs and dialogues.

But later, she was surprised when she heard what Neeli Akkan said. Neither Parvathi nor Ganga nor the Queen nor the rest of the actresses were women. They were all men in disguise. *Can the men transform themselves to become such beautiful women?* No woman had ever done a role in Kakkarissi plays before, Neeli Akkan added.

The Parvathi whom Rosy saw in the Kakkarissi play refused to leave her mind. Often when Rosy was sure that there was no one around, she would pretend to be Parvathi or Kakkalathi or Vettuvathi and sing and dance like them. Near her hut, there was a lonely bush on the side of the pond. This was where she did her acting.

'Thatha, thikathi thakatha, they they, thatha...'

She danced while singing the song that rose on the stage when Parvathi first appears in a Kakkarissi performance. Then pretending to be Kakkalathi who reads the King's palm, she thundered out the fiery speeches that Kakkalathi made against the forces of the dark and the demons. Holding a small piece of mirror near her face to see her changing expressions, she enjoyed the emotions and dialogues all by herself.

One evening she was in full flow, enacting the role of Parvathi by the lakeside. She had just taken a breath after delivering a passionate speech when she heard a clap and a firm voice congratulating her, saying, 'Koche, that was brilliant!'

Rosy was amazed. She turned her head in the direction of the sound. At first, she could not see anyone. The next moment a man came into view from behind a huge jackfruit tree. He must have been more than sixty, but with a firm body and bright eyes. He was dressed in a white mundu with a towel folded across his shoulders.

Rosy felt that she had seen the man somewhere before. That too very recently. Nor was this an ordinary meeting. That was definite. By then he had reached very near her.

'Girl, who taught you how to perform in Kakkarissi plays?'

Hearing his question, Rosy turned pale. *Didn't Neeli Akkan say that girls should not play or are not allowed to play Kakkarissi? Did I break that custom? What if the news gets around that a Christian—that too a Dalit—has broken the custom of Hindus?* She trembled at the thought.

'Ayyo, I was simply mimicking it...I haven't studied anything,' she stammered.

'Hey penne, why be afraid? What you played just now was Kakkarissi. It was well played too. Ha, my name is Govindan. I'm a Kakkarissi Asan.'

Next, Asan acted out the humiliation and distress that had played on Rosy's face in that moment. He laughed out loudly. Watching his acting, his pupils who had also arrived at the spot by then joined in the laughter. His humour was so infectious that it was not possible to take offence. Rosy protested mildly, 'Enough of this, Asan! Don't make such fun of poor people like me.'

So, the day before going to see Daniel Sir, Rosy made her way to the Kalari to obtain permission and blessings from Asan. With Asan were some new students who had come to learn Kakkarissi. All boys.

Govindan Asan was telling the students the story of how he found and trained Rosy to be the first actress in the history of Kakkarissi. It was a chapter in her life that Rosy could never forget. First the resistance from Rosy's house, then the opposition from the Kakkarissi performers (especially the men who used to dress up and play Parvathi), above all the plucky support from Asan due to which she could overcome everything and get on the stage after two years of hard practice. Then the dance steps she performed as the beloved Kakkalathi for the Kakkarissi lovers on umpteen stages around Trivandrum, in the Kalari, Asan preparing good food for her—she was in poor health because of the straitened circumstances at home, especially before Paulose got a job as a cook in LMS—for she needed a strong, resilient body to perform Kakkarissi the whole night; Asan standing resolutely behind her to bring her back on stage when she was about to quit after listening to rumours about them spread by some jealous people. How many such scenes about Asan were there?

Lifting up Rosy, who had fallen at his feet, Govindan Asan said, 'Girl, you will reach many heights. It was really the Lord Nataraja who chose me to turn you into an artist. This happiness that it was I who found you! Enough, that is enough for me.'

As Rosy was getting ready to leave after bidding goodbye to the Kalari, Asan laughed out loud. Rosy looked at him in amazement. Neither she nor Asan nor anyone had said anything to trigger that laugh. Observing the query in her face, Asan smilingly said, 'Suddenly I remembered something. Previously when you began this play, you used to pray to your Jesus Christ with some distress. Now when you act in movies, you can pray to Jesus without any misgivings. The god of cinema would not be Shiva, but your Christ himself.' Now Rosy too laughed.

That was the biggest problem that Rosy had had when she used to perform in the Kakkarissi. Before going on stage, each artist would pray silently to Lord Shiva that they be able to play well. It was believed that if they did so, it would have a positive effect upon their performance.

But Rosy could not even think of praying to another god and forsaking her Jesus. Thus, every time, she would go on stage after praying to Jesus.

Once, while performing, Rosy missed her steps two or three times for which she got a good scolding from Asan. Despondently, Rosy thought about why she was making so many mistakes.

Finally, she figured out the reason: *I am getting on stage after praying to Jesus rather than to Shiva. These mistakes are the punishments given to me by Him*. She was overcome with guilt.

After some days Rosy presented her plight before Govindan Asan. At first Asan listened to what she was saying seriously. He did not speak for some time. Rosy's heart was beating in anxiety. Then Asan said, 'Girl, this is a very big problem indeed. You are showing great disregard for the gods.'

A tremor spread through Rosy.

Then Govindan Asan burst out laughing. Rosy stood wide-eyed. After laughing heartily for a few moments, Asan said, 'Girl, I was simply making fun of you. The art that we perform in earnest is our prayer. In that there is no difference between Shiva or Jesus. Perform your art sincerely, whichever god you pray to.'

The next day everyone told Rosy that her performance the night before was fabulous.

The smile on Asan's face did not vanish even after Rosy walked away. Her guru's blessing remained in her heart as a revitalizing prayer.

THREE

A BULLOCK CART belonging to one of Johnson's acquaintances was going via Pattom. As the driver was the sole occupant, there was enough space for Johnson Sir and Rosy to travel with him.

This was the first time in her eighteen years that Rosy was travelling by a cart. Nor had she ever gone to Pattom.

As the cart shuddered its way forward, her gaze fell upon the sights of the town through a hole at the rear of the cart. It was morning, and the street was crowded. Horse carts made their way at a smart trot through the crowds. Hajur Kacheri and VJT Hall appeared before Rosy's eyes and bid a fast retreat.

Rosy was feeling quite embarrassed travelling

with a strange man, and that too someone from the upper class. But other than asking some questions every now and again about Kakkarissi, Johnson did not pay much attention to her. This increased her regard for him.

Rosy remembered how she was the target of lewd stares and loose talk from men in big houses when she went out for manual work. If the women in the houses were out of sight, they would try to strike up a conversation and make suggestive gestures. *In contrast, how respectfully Johnson Sir behaves!*

The bullock cart stopped when it reached a bungalow near a hill in Pattom. After getting out from the cart Johnson pointed to the bungalow and said, 'Look, that is Saradavilasam Building. Daniel's studio and office are there.'

Saradavilasam was a bungalow with clean walls painted white and a large pebbled courtyard where a few mango trees bloomed. The name 'Saradavilasam' was carved on the wall of the portico near the entrance of the building. On a wooden board beside that was written 'The Travancore National Pictures.'

After asking Rosy to sit on a chair in a tall, wide room, Johnson went to another room at the end of the building. That room was Daniel's office.

Rosy looked around wide-eyed. A cool breeze

blew in through the large open windows. She thought with astonishment that this was the first time she was entering such a big bungalow.

In a few minutes, Johnson invited Rosy to Daniel Sir's room.

'Daniel, this is Rosy. My neighbour,' Johnson said to Daniel with a smile.

Timidly, Rosy greeted Daniel by folding both her hands together. Even in that state of apprehension, her eyes took in appreciatively the firm body and the handsome, expressive face of Daniel. Though she could see only a small part of him sitting across a table in a big chair, she could tell that this was an unusually handsome and well-built young man.

'Oh, come in, come and sit down,' Daniel invited both of them to the chairs across his table. Though Johnson sat immediately, she hesitated.

'Girl, be seated,' said Daniel with a small smile. But Rosy stood indecisively.

Then Johnson intervened. 'Look, this is our director, which means the director of the movie. He is also the producer. The all-in-all of this movie. You have to obey everything he says if you are to work in his movie. How can you defy him? Come here and sit down.'

Rosy sat down on the chair in great embarrassment. She knew that Daniel was watching her closely. Some minutes passed in silence.

Then Daniel asked, 'Rosy, have you ever seen a movie?'

'No Sir, I have not.'

She had heard that there was a theatre in Trivandrum called Capitol. It was somewhere near the Hajur Kacheri. She had heard that Tamil, Hindi and English films were brought from other lands and shown there. But she had never been inside it herself.

Daniel looked at her with a silent smile. But since it was not the usual leering sort of look that she was used to from men, she did not feel angry at all. Not only that—his cool gaze, which radiated a purity similar to the spotless white shirt he was wearing, allowed her a peace of mind that brimmed with courage too.

Then, the sound of Daniel's voice rang out. 'Rosy, stand up.'

She got up immediately.

'I'll describe a scene to you. You act it out. Hmm? Imagine that you are in love with a man. You are walking in front of your house. Suddenly that man appears before you. At that time, you feel bashful love for him, happiness and surprise all at once. That is the scene.'

For a second Rosy closed her eyes and prayed to God. Then she let the words that Daniel said flow into her heart. She had never felt love for a man till then. Not even for John from Amathara with whom her marriage had previously been fixed. Yet any girl in the ripeness of youth would know within her heart what love is.

Rosy opened her eyes and looked intensely at Daniel's face. The one standing before her now is not her master Daniel, but a young man, masculine enough to attract any young girl. Rosy is only a girl standing lovelorn in front of that young man.

In a flash, the emotions of a lovesick girl flickered one after the other on Rosy's face.

'Right, that's enough,' Daniel's words shattered the imaginary world that she had just entered. Rosy looked at Daniel and Johnson, a trifle embarrassed.

'Rosy, can you wait outside for some time?'

Rosy left the room. Standing near the window of the drawing room, she looked outside. Two squirrels were playing on the branches of the mango tree in the front yard. She tried to concentrate on the squirrels though she knew that Daniel was discussing her with Johnson. *I will soon know if I will act in this movie or not. God! The squirrels are playing without a care. If only men could think of their lives too as a game! Perhaps the game of human life is an assortment of anxiety, hopes and disappointments...*

'Rosy, come in,' Johnson's voice came to her from the inner room.

With a thumping heart, she entered Daniel's room.

'Look, you are no longer ordinary Rosy. From now on, you are filmstar Rosy.'

There was a teasing smile on Daniel Sir's face.

She stood still, wide-eyed.

'Didn't you understand, Rosy? You are the heroine in my new film. Let's do this well, shall we?'

A stunned Rosy just smiled.

Daniel continued, 'We've decided on a salary of five rupees per day for you. You have the role of Sarojini, a Nair girl, and we will give you the costume for the role. Well, do you agree?' Rosy nodded her head, still smiling. *Do I agree! Appan gets ten rupees a month for working in the kitchen of the white missionary. Now five rupees for a day's work! It's true what they say about cinema. It's indeed a big thing.*

When she went back to Thycaud, Johnson was not with her. He stayed behind as he had something to discuss with Daniel.

The afternoon sun was blazing hot. Yet she did not feel the heat.

This Rosy who is now walking towards Thycaud is not the poor Pulaya girl Rosy. This is Rosy, the first heroine of Malayalam cinema. But even now I don't know what cinema is. I know it is a big thing. And I am the most important person in that big thing.

A horse cart that was rushing past narrowly missed her. The driver shouted at her. But Rosy carried on, oblivious to everything.

FOUR

THE DRAWING ROOM of Saradavilasam is now a grand, traditional Nair tharavad. Rosy is now Sarojini, the only girl of the house. She is bedecked like any other girl of a majestic tharavad—in an expensive mundu and blouse; adorned with gold ornaments on her neck, ears, hands and feet.

Sitting in the portico, Sarojini is happily playing the veena. Then a handsome young man named Jayachandran, who is passing by, sees her for the first time. He stands fascinated, watching her. After some time, she meets the gaze of the young man. Even at that first sight, they are attracted to each other...it is the blossoming of a love story.

This is the first scene in which Rosy is going to

act. Daniel is acting as Jayachandran. Now he is giving some instructions to the Malaysian cameraman named Lalan. They are discussing the scene in detail.

The day before, during the rehearsal, Daniel had explained to Rosy in detail about the plot and the character she was to portray. When she heard all that for the first time, she felt afraid. *I don't know how girls from big Nair tharavads walk or do things... And the heroine of the film is someone who is adept at playing the veena—I have never even touched a veena...*

But Daniel just said, 'Don't you worry. Just act like a smart girl, which means just like you. Then everything will be all right.'

He showed her how to hold the veena and play it. 'Rosy, this is cinema. No one here has come to appreciate you playing the veena. People watching you should feel that you are playing it. That's all. Just act,' laughed Daniel.

Yet now that she was in the front of the camera for the first time, she felt scared. *God, please help me.*

'Okay. Start.' Daniel's voice rang out.

Rosy placed the veena on her lap and started playing on it as directed by Daniel. She knew that discordant notes were rising. But, discerning that it did not matter, she started acting like Sarojini who was engrossed in her music.

Within minutes, Jayachandran walked by the window. Their eyes met. Embarrassment on Sarojini's face, shyness, their mutual attraction.

The camera copied the scene just as it was in Daniel's imagination.

'Cut,' Daniel's voice came again. 'Well done, Rosy, well done.'

Rosy stood still for a minute, hearing the English words. *What does this mean?*

'It was good, Rosy. Good. You really became Sarojini.'

A full smile on Daniel's face. Her eyes filled with tears. *Oh God, Sir is satisfied with the first piece of my acting.*

Johnson, who was staying away from the camera's eye, came towards her. 'You saved my reputation. If the heroine I brought for Daniel was bad, I would have had it. Now your success is mine too.'

'Ayyo, spare some credit for the director too,' Daniel called out. Johnson laughed loudly.

Though she felt happy that everyone was satisfied with her acting, she was surprised at one thing. Compared to the Kakkarissi acting, where one had to act a whole night using one's whole body, acting in the cinema was so easy. It could be done just by small movements and emotions on the face. For the Kakkarissi play, the actor needed so much training to get one's act perfect.

Not only that, in Kakkarissi you act directly in front of an audience. If there is something amiss, the result will be known then and there. But here, in cinema, there are many chances to set right anything that may go wrong.

As she bit into the sweet mango that had fallen from the tree in the yard while the next shot was being prepared, Rosy sighed. *Ha, anyway I will know how my acting is when the movie comes out.*

After that scene, more shots were taken with Sarojini, her mother and Sarojini's friend Hemavathy. An Ehzava lady called Kamala from Kunnukuzhi donned the role of the mother, and a Pulaya girl called Reena was Hemavathy. She too was from Kunnukuzhi.

Moments after they were introduced to each other, Kamala had told Rosy the story of her life. Kamala had four children. Her husband drank away all the money he got as daily wages. Given a chance, he would take away the money that Kamala also got as her wages, to spend on drink. In short, they lived in utter poverty, when she came to know from her neighbour Pachu Annan that they were looking for a woman to do a role in cinema. Pachu Annan was the tailor who stitched costumes for cinema, and so the cinema people would give some credence to his recommendations. That is how Kamala came to cinema.

But Kamala's husband would create havoc if he heard about her acting in the cinema. She came to Saradavilasam after telling him that she was going to work in some house.

'But Chechi, if he comes to know later that you had gone to act in movies, won't that create a problem?' Rosy asked.

'Oh, that is much later. I will see to it when it comes to that,' Kamala said with a smirk.

As they had never acted before in their lives, Kamala and Reena often made mistakes. But Daniel slowly corrected their acting through patient guidance.

In the afternoon Rosy, Kamala and Reena sat on a mat on the floor and ate their lunch. Daniel and Johnson ate sitting in the inner room.

Of the three women, Rosy brought the best food. Kamala and Reena had only some boiled asparagus and chilly chutney. Rosy had more gruel in her box than she wanted. She poured some of it on to

Kamala and Reena's plates. Though they refused at first, they happily drank what she gave them.

Before the afternoon's shoot, while they rested on the same mat, Kamala imparted some news about the story behind this cinema.

'It was tailor Pachu Anna who told me all these things. Rosy, do you know who was actually supposed to do your role?' Kamala spat out betel juice dramatically. Rosy looked at her anxiously.

'It was an Anglo-Indian beauty called Lana from Bombay.' After giving this bit of information, Kamala again inserted something into her mouth and started chewing. Rosy could not contain her surprise. 'Chechi, then how come I was called?'

Kamala spat out the betel juice again in a long arc and continued: 'Daniel Sir is the son of a rich doctor belonging to the Nadar caste. After his college studies he became mad about cinema. He went to Madras and Bombay to learn how to make films. Then he tried to make a movie by himself, and formed a cinema company and constructed a studio by selling most of his ancestral property.

'Though he could arrange for everything else, he could not get a heroine even after hunting for long. He put out advertisements in the newspaper. But no one was willing to send their girls to act in a movie.

'In the end an Anglo-Indian girl called Lana or somebody from Bombay expressed willingness to be the heroine. She was a real beauty. But she would come only if she was given a huge amount of money. It is heard that her salary was decided at five thousand rupees. Daniel Sir agreed to everything, and he himself went and brought her in a train from Bombay to Trivandrum with all the facilities she demanded.

'But she made a lot of fuss. She insisted that she will come only in a car from the railway station in Pettah to the building where she was to stay. Wouldn't budge an inch even when they told her that the horse cart arranged for her was good. Having no other option, Daniel Sir finally brought a car for her.

'As she was travelling in that car in great style, she saw some grand buildings on the way. One of the buildings caught her fancy. Do you know which that was? Kowdiar Palace where our King stayed. Then and there she started a hue and cry. She wanted to stay there itself and not in any other building. Daniel Sir pleaded with her, but she stuck to her foolishness. If anyone else had heard about it, they would have given her a thrashing.

'Suffice it to say, eventually Daniel Sir somehow

managed to put her on the next train to Bombay. But she left without repaying even a pie of what she took as advance from him. All this happened around one and a half years ago. By that time most of the parts in which the heroine did not appear had been shot. After that, Sir and everyone else with him started frantically searching for a heroine.

'What to say Rosy, it was destined for you. Even after searching all over Bombay, he couldn't find anyone because it was fated that a girl from Thycaud would do the role.'

Just then came Daniel's voice calling Rosy for the next shot. She got up and swiftly walked to the shooting location.

Even as one part of Rosy's brain was listening to Daniel explaining the importance of the next scene, the other part was deep in thought about what she had just heard from Kamala.

She had felt happy when Johnson came and asked her if she could do the role and later when Daniel decided to hire her. But she did not know at that time that what she was going to do was such a big thing. *Am I not that rarest of women who could not be found even after searching the whole country? Am I not playing a role that no one could do even when they were promised a large amount of money? And for me, mere five rupees as wages, no train or horse cart or bullock cart, only walking on my bare feet...*

But at the very next moment she reined in her thoughts. *Oh God, what am I thinking? They chose me as a heroine by God's grace. Not only that, I had not seen a whole five-rupee currency note all my life. In this grand town, I am only a poor unknown girl living in the corner. Yet, is my heart going wayward now that it has heard the story of big money and tantrums born of luxury? Am I finding fault with Daniel Sir who has shown me only kindness and love?*

She took a decision that from then on, she would not let her mind wander to thoughts about money.

Within minutes she transformed herself totally into Sarojini. The next scene was that Jayachandran comes to Sarojini's house and meets her parents. After that, everyone listens to Sarojini playing the veena. Gradually Jayachandran and Sarojini grow closer.

For all these scenes Daniel had written dialogues in a high-flown dialect. But as it was a silent movie, Daniel had told them not to worry too much about the dialogue. Hearing this, Rosy and Kamala lost their fear. They only had to move their lips as if they were talking, and the camera would capture it.

When the light waned, Daniel consulted Lalan and decided to stop shooting for the day.

Johnson had told her that shooting can be done only when there is bright light. In Bombay, they had lights that ran on electricity to help in shooting. If such lights were available, there was no need for sunlight. But, in Trivandrum, electricity was only just coming into use. So such lights were not in vogue. That was also the reason why Daniel was trying to complete the shooting before the rains started.

The ladies' room was just near Daniel's office. All the beautiful dresses and ornaments for the characters were kept there. They were supposed to wear these each day when they came for the shooting.

As she changed into her own dress, Rosy told herself: *Now I have turned into a Pulaya girl again. Only tomorrow will I again become Sarojini, the grand Nair girl...*

FIVE

ROSY REACHED HOME in the fading light, gazing on the way at the big buildings by the roadside, at people rushing hither and thither in the evenings and at the eight-seater steam bus coming from Kollam to Trivandrum. Paulose had not yet returned from the white missionary's house. He usually came home late after preparing dinner there.

Kunji and Mala were waiting for Rosy to come home. As soon as she saw Rosy, Mala started asking her about cinema. Rosy was unable to take even a sip of the black coffee that Kunji had kept for her, as Mala plied her with questions.

Kunji became anxious when she came to know that Rosy was acting as a Nair girl. She said, 'Won't the thamburans get angry when they hear that a Pulaya girl is doing the role of a Nair? Remember what happened during Kakkarissi! I don't know what you are up to now...'

'Mother, what's wrong with you? Why do you have to be so afraid? This is just acting. What have the thamburans got to do with it?' Rosy asked as she sipped her coffee.

Mala could not get enough of cinema news. It was only when her mother Velutha called her that she half-heartedly left Rosy.

When Paulose came home, Rosy shared her cinema news once more with him. After he heard everything he said, 'I told the white man about your cinema. He says that back in America, heroines, actresses, are all in good positions. The ministers and presidents who rule the country look at the heroes and heroines with great respect. Oh God, will our child too become like that...?'

'If that is so then after I finish acting in this movie, our Regent Queen may come and visit me, alle?' Rosy asked, in all seriousness. Kunji and Paulose looked at her awestruck. She held on to her serious act for a moment more. Then she burst out laughing. 'You got scared, right? You thought I put on airs all of a sudden?'

Now Paulose too joined in her laughter. He said, 'Our daughter belongs to the heritage of Kotharani. There is nothing surprising about all this, Kunji.'

'Oh yes,' Kunji smirked. Seeing this, Rosy burst out laughing again. Kotharani was a name that crept in on those few occasions when her father and mother quarrelled.

The story went that many, many years ago a Pulaya queen named Kotha ruled over a place called Kokkothamangalam near Nedumangad. She was also called Kokkotharani. It was said that Rosy's father's family had descended from her. That was why her father boasted of Kotharani's ancestry whenever he picked quarrels with her mother.

Now Rosy went and sat near Kunji and said with a lisp, 'So now you are the Queen Mother of Rosy the Queen, isn't she, Appan?'

Kunji just looked at her sternly and blew into the fire below the boiling pot of gruel.

The shooting for the next day consisted of scenes with Sarojini, Jayachandran and Jayachandran's friend Chandrakumar. In these scenes the intimacy between Jayachandran and Sarojini grew further. They fell in love.

While the shooting was going on, some of Daniel's friends paid a visit. They were all praise for

Rosy's acting as they watched her following Daniel's instructions.

One of them said in awe: 'Hey, from where did you get this girl, Daniel? You were telling us you searched in all the Nair households but couldn't find anyone! From which tharavadu did you get her?'

Rosy was wiping the sweat off her face after the shot when she heard this. She turned her head and looked at Daniel's friend.

What did he say? He thinks that I'm from some illustrious Nair tharavad! I only had to wear good clothes and some jewellery and I am no longer a poor Pulaya girl! So, what others say is right—that unlike other Pulaya girls I am fair-skinned and beautiful. Rosy blushed.

Hearing what his friend said, Daniel looked at Rosy. He winked at her with a smile and said, 'Ha! At last the elders from one tharavad agreed.'

Another friend asked Rosy, 'Which is your tharavad?'

Rosy turned pale.

Daniel patted the interrogator's shoulder and remarked jokingly, 'Edo, don't cook trouble by enquiring after her tharavad. They are illustrious people. They will not want any association with good-for-nothings like you. So, mister, better stay away.'

Deeply embarrassed, the man managed to hide it by joining in everybody's laughter. Rosy too joined in, laughing.

Now she felt she was acting for real. She felt surprised that after becoming a film actress she could act so well in life too.

When all his friends had left after lunch, Daniel called Rosy to his room. He was alone.

After Daniel had asked her repeatedly to sit on the chair, she did. Daniel sat looking at her for a second. Then his face broke into a smile.

'Rosy, you heard what my friends said when they came, didn't you? Asking who this Nair girl was? Indeed! They really think you are one. Nor did I correct them. For the time being let them think whatever they want. At least until we finish shooting our film, let them not know that it's a Pulaya girl who dons the role of a Nair. That will be better. You don't have a problem with that, do you?'

'Oh no, Sir. But when they hear my name is Rosy, won't they wonder how a Nair girl got such a name?'

'That's true. But they will think that it is your name for the movies. Even in foreign countries film actresses use other names.'

'Acting in the movies and out of it, alle, Sir?' Rosy asked softly, a new understanding in her voice.

Daniel looked at her closely. Rosy felt that she had done something wrong.

A mocking smile appeared on Daniel's face. 'Rosy, do you know how lucky you are that you were not born a Nair or Nadar girl? Do you know how hard I searched for a good-looking girl who could act the role of Sarojini? But not a single one would come. They think that acting is a disreputable job. Good for you that you don't come from such a background. Good for me too.'

So what Kamala said was true. What if I ask Daniel Sir about the actress from Bombay now? But Rosy let the thought go, thinking that he would be offended.

As she was leaving after her day's shoot, Daniel told her that she did not have any scenes for the next four days and so she need not come during those days.

'And remember not to go for any other job and ruin my heroine's beauty. We need you as beautiful as this till the movie is finished,' he smiled.

The walk back home through the town after work had become very dear to Rosy. That day, as she started her walk, she felt a bit gloomy thinking she would not be coming back that way for some days.

The esteemed members of society who came out

for an evening stroll on the royal streets; those who travelled accompanied by the jingling of bells in the jadkas and bullock carts; those who returned after work from the Hajur Kacheri; those coming back from the market; huge houses where the rich stayed—it was fun to watch all this on the walk back home. Rosy had especially noticed some houses on the street. Not only the houses, but also the well-dressed, beflowered happy young women there. Mostly Nair girls. Women who lived their lives in luxury, without a care in the world. *How will they know the difficulty with which girls like me get on with our lives?*

But today when Rosy saw the houses and the girls, it was Daniel's words that echoed in her mind.

'Rosy, do you know how lucky you are that you were not born a Nair or Nadar girl?'

It was only because I was a Pulaya girl that I was able to act in this movie. Girls in rich houses and of high caste may have good clothes, jewellery and rich food, but in a way they are like birds kept in a cage. In a golden cage. Just because these women have money, an illustrious ancestry and are from a high caste, they are not free. There may be many among them who have talents for singing, dancing or acting. But at the most what they could do is to enjoy playing the veena at home. That is all.

Like Sarojini.

Suddenly she stopped walking and stood transfixed on the road. *Yes, the Sarojini I carry in my heart and soul. She is one of them whom I look at in longing; she belongs to one of these rich houses.*

I was happy that I was one of them when I was dressed up as Sarojini. I also felt proud when one of Daniel Sir's friends mistook me for one of them. Yes, pride.

Now I don't feel pride but sympathy. I was feeling proud to be a girl who could not work for art even when she was interested in it. I was feeling great about becoming a girl who—though very talented—found it demeaning to become an artist.

And I? Appan allowed me to act in the Kakkarissi when I told him I wanted to. That too at a time when no woman had ever ventured to step in there. He never blamed me even when the Kakkarissi people and the drama people fomented trouble for me and we had to move out of the house to a new one. Only Ammachi uttered some bitter words. But I know that she said it out of the pain in her heart.

Ever since I was a child, I have had an irrepressible desire to dance and sing and enact roles. How many times have I acted out different characters from the stories that I learned in my third standard in front of the broken piece of mirror at home? When no one was looking, I liked to make up dialogues and say them in front of the mirror. Later when I saw Kakkarissi, acting became part of my life.

It would have been really sad if people at home had not allowed me to act when this movie offer presented itself, because I was so passionate about it. In a way, it was only because I was a poor Pulaya girl that I could enter cinema.

As Rosy resumed walking, she heard a veena being played in one of the big houses. When you heard it, you knew it was an experienced hand that was playing the veena so marvellously.

But Rosy did not wait to listen to it. Some days back, she would have. But now she knew that it was some unlucky girl who was the veena player.

Rosy walked on with a stronger sense of freedom and pride than ever before. It was not just the pride of having become a heroine, but it was a walk that was filled with the pride and happiness of having been born a Pulaya girl—steps that were filled with the happiness of an unchained Pulaya.

Some of the eminent people who were walking by and others passing in all their jadkas' grandeur, looked in surprise at this woman walking with such unusually confident body language. Rosy did not feel clumsy like before when men had leered at her. Her body did not shrink in a feeling of inferiority. She kept treading the road firmly, striding ahead in her own rapture.

SIX

THE NEXT DAY Rosy had thought that she would just sit around the house doing nothing. But when Appan and Amma had gone out for work, Mala brought some exciting news.

There was some work to be done in the compound of a huge tharavad beside Karamana river. Apart from other work, there was overgrown grass to be cut too. Whichever way you looked at it, by the time dusk came to settle, you would have at least five chakrams* in your hand.

Even after hearing what Mala said, Rosy just

*Coin prevalent in the old Travancore kingdom. Twenty-eight chakrams would be the equivalent of one rupee.

yawned and stretched before sitting down on the mattress.

'Hmm? Why, don't you like what I said? Oh, maybe cinema actresses will not do menial jobs or cut grass...' Mala smirked.

'Go away or you'll get it from me,' Rosy made as if to beat Mala.

'I was just letting you know. If Madam Film Actress does not want to come, you may do as you wish.'

Actually, Rosy had taken to heart what Daniel had told her about keeping herself beautiful till the film shooting was finished. She did not want to get dark skin from the heat of the sun, or hurt herself with some sickle working outdoors. On the other hand, she also did not want to make her best friend angry. Though Mala was merely joking now, there was a chance that she may take this seriously.

It would be a shame if Mala thinks I'm proud just because I've become a film actress. Who knows about cinema? Will I get to work in another movie after this, or will another movie itself be produced again? Who knows? Then would I not have to return to my old life with a spade, broom and sickle? It is better to go with Mala now.

'Well, okay lass, let's not lose your opportunity

to work with a film actress,' Rosy said, pinching Mala's cheek.

What Mala said was right. There was a lot of overgrown grass in the grounds alongside the river. Mala and Rosy decided to start weeding and grass-cutting and finish as early as they could, following the instructions of Sivan Pillai, the overseer at the tharavad who gave them work elsewhere too.

As their work proceeded, Pillai as usual began to find fault with the female workers and shout at them. He would not be at peace until he did that. But Rosy could not go on working with her head lowered as he wanted. Before, even when she knew that he was unnecessarily shouting at them, she had never felt angry. But now she was disturbed by his shouting. *Am I to bear all this nonsense again?* But Rosy quickly swallowed her anger.

After finishing the weeding work, Mala had started to cut the grass. But Rosy was far behind in her work. Usually when they cut grass, Mala could never match Rosy's pace.

Mala queried, 'Hmm? Why are you so woebegone?'

Though she said it was nothing, Rosy knew that Mala's question rang true.

There is some change in me...Earlier it was fun competing with Mala while cutting grass. But after the cinema and the acting, I am not able to give myself up wholly to weeding and cutting grass. It is only three days since I was in the world of movies. Is acting and the recognition I got from Daniel Sir changing me from being the old Rosy? Oh God, let me not forget anything.

Rosy prayed as she cut the grass. Mala had started singing a Tamil drama song which was in vogue with gusto. Rosy too tried to join in, humming the song along with her.

The next two days, Rosy went along with Mala for work.

When the day's work was over, and she was returning from the Manakkad market after selling the grass, she saw Johnson. It was the day before she had to resume acting. Seeing him, she felt embarrassed. *Just looking at my muddied body, covered with sweat, one can make out that I am returning from work in the fields.* Though she tried to slip away, Rosy could not manage to get away in time.

'Who is this? Our heroine?'

Rosy's face flushed in shame. She looked at Mala through the corner of her eye. Mala was standing near her, openly smiling at Johnson.

'I will definitely inform Daniel about this, ketto—that our heroine is loitering in town with baskets and sickles, eh?'

'Johnson Sir, er...' Rosy searched for the right word. She felt uneasy and embarrassed. Daniel had told her not to go to work for the time being. *And here I am...*

Seeing the anxiety on Rosy's face, Johnson shook off his seriousness. 'Ayyo, girl, don't worry. I was just pulling your leg. To tell the truth, what you are doing now is the right thing. There are those who grow arrogant thinking that they have become actresses and beyond these things. They should learn from you. You are doing your job sincerely, be it manual labour or acting in the movies...You are not trying to be a lady just because you acted in a film. This is what you should do.'

Rosy looked at him in wonder.

'Yes girl, what I said is the truth.' He waved as he walked away into a by-lane to Thampanoor: 'Well, see you in the studio tomorrow.'

Johnson's praise gave much solace to Rosy. *In one way, this is the answer to the thoughts that have plagued me the whole day...*

SEVEN

THE NEXT DAY, when Rosy was walking towards Pattom, she suddenly heard an uproar: the sound of horse hoofs approaching, of people shouting, and the honk of a motor vehicle. She moved towards the roadside and turned to watch the spectacle.

It was the Regent Queen. She was coming from the Satelmond palace in Mudavanmugal to pay a visit to the Sri Padmanabhaswamy temple. She was sitting in an open car, escorted by soldiers on horseback who rode in front and behind.

This was the first time that Rosy was witnessing the Queen's journey at such close quarters. Usually, the lower-caste people never stood anywhere near the retinue on the royal path.

Rosy stood there watching the procession. The car in which the Queen was sitting passed by close to her. She felt the Queen's gaze on her body.

Hey! I forgot to bow and pay my respects to the Queen! The usual custom is to bow reverentially before the royal men and women as they pass by like this. There seems to be a slight hint of wonder on the Queen's face...Was she aghast at the sight of an outcaste girl, standing freely and arrogantly in front of her retinue, even after she saw it approaching? But is it possible to recognize that I am low-caste at a glance? People say otherwise.

Chee! Why should I bother myself thinking about all this? I am an actress now. According to Govindan Asan, acting is a noble art. For anyone practising it, things like caste should never be an issue. In front of art, there is no caste or untouchability.

Rosy walked on with added vigour.

Even from afar, Rosy noticed that the studio and its surroundings were festooned with streamers and other decorations. *What is special today? Maybe there are certain scenes to be shot today that need such decorations.*

Soon, she came to learn that it was all done for certain special guests. Janet, Daniel's wife, had come to watch the shoot, along with her two little kids.

Rosy, dressed up as Sarojini, watched Janet with curiosity. Janet was sitting on a chair and talking to Daniel, who was getting dressed up as Jayachandran. The glances they exchanged and the way they spoke to each other exuded love.

Janet is really very beautiful! A perfect match for Daniel Sir. Kamala said they fell in love when they were quite young. No wonder, they really make such a perfect couple.

The kids were playing in and around the studio premises. The elder son, Sundaram, was four years old. He played the main role in the film, that of Chandrakumar in his childhood. He was the son who was kidnapped by the villains and taken to Ceylon. The daughter, Sulochana, was two years old and played the role of Sarojini in her childhood. Thus, Sundaram and Sulochana, brother and sister in real life, played the role of the siblings in the story, Chandrakumar and Sarojini. It seemed that the scenes of the children had already been captured by the camera.

By lunchtime, Rosy and Janet had become very close. With great interest, Janet had enquired about matters relating to Rosy's family and her acting in Kakkarissi plays. When she came to know that Rosy's father worked in the kitchen of the missionary sayip at LMS, she said: 'Oho, then I have definitely had dinner prepared by your father. Two months back, the sayip had hosted a dinner for some families here including ours. Let me tell you, the food was really tasty.'

When Sulochana came and climbed on to Janet's lap, she said to her daughter, 'Look, this Rosy Chechi is the one who plays the grown-up character of the girl's role you had played in the cinema.' Bemused, Sulochana looked at Rosy. *Who knows if the kid understood anything?*

After having her lunch with Daniel, Janet came to the mango tree under which Rosy, Kamala and Reena were resting. She told them a little apologetically, 'Ayyo, when I left home in the morning, I didn't know there will be a few women like you here. Otherwise I would have brought some fish fry or something with me. Do you all eat fish and meat?'

When all three stood without uttering a word, Janet laughed: 'Don't feel uneasy. I will be coming tomorrow also. Then I will bring some mutton fry and fish curry.' This time around, Kamala said, 'Ayyo, Madam, don't take so much trouble about us like this.'

'Trouble? This shooting is going to last only for

a few more days. After that, I won't be able to meet you all,' Janet said, as she lifted up Sulochana, who had come running to her after a fight with Sundaram.

When Janet left them, Kamala said with a long sigh, 'Ayyo, me and Reena are really unlucky. We don't have work tomorrow. So you'll get all the delicacies Janet Madam brings tomorrow. You are really lucky.'

Hearing that, Rosy felt sad. In that case, should they ask her to bring the special dishes when Kamala and Reena were there? When they heard Rosy's idea, Kamala put her finger on her nose, 'Hey, dearie, what are you saying? Who are we to tell Madam to bring the dishes on this day or that? You keep quiet. And tomorrow eat whatever she brings for us too.'

Before it was evening, they had to shoot the scenes where Jayachandran, riding a bicycle, plucks a flower from Sarojini's hair and kisses it. It was followed by scenes where they exchange smiles and glances of love.

Rosy was a little perturbed thinking about how to act out such a love scene with Daniel when Janet was watching. Because of that, during the rehearsals before the take, there were many errors in her behaviour and movements. Daniel was upset watching Rosy make so many mistakes, which was unusual. He looked at her with a little uneasiness: 'What is this, Rosy? You are distracted.'

But Janet, who was watching the shoot, understood the reason. She had noticed Rosy giving her embarrassed glances during the shoot.

Janet went up to Daniel and said, 'Look, the reason is that Rosy is embarrassed because I am here. She is worried about how to play these love scenes with you when I am looking.'

Daniel looked at Janet in amazement. 'How did you know that?'

'Women easily make out such things,' Janet smiled.

Daniel called Rosy to him, and asked whether what Janet told him was true.

Rosy's face blushed in embarrassment. She looked at Janet and smiled timidly. Janet lightly patted Rosy's cheeks. 'Look, koche, this is only acting. You go ahead and act, love. Don't bother about me at all.'

The rehearsal resumed. Rosy quickly regained her usual prowess in acting. Once Janet told her she did not mind the scenes, her bashfulness and embarrassment disappeared.

Once the shooting of the love scenes was over, Janet came to Rosy and grasped her hands: 'Beautiful, really beautiful! I wonder whether even I have looked at Daniel with so much love till now. Listen, you really loved.'

Then Daniel said, 'When she looked at me like that with so much love, I too felt love for her! Am I in trouble, Janet?'

Janet laughed and pinched Daniel on his cheek.

Johnson, who was watching all this, joined with an exaggeratedly pathetic look on his face. 'Rosy, don't put me in trouble. In the end, I will get beaten up by Janet. It was I who brought you here, isn't it?'

Everyone laughed. Rosy smiled, but her face paled with embarrassment.

Then Janet said, 'Okay, no more comments from anyone. If we offend our heroine, we only stand to lose by that.'

Next morning, they were shooting the scene where Viswamohan, friend of the main villain of the story, Bhoothanathan, tries to molest Sarojini. The scene was to be shot in a garden near the studio. Sarojini is strolling alone in the garden. Viswamohan, who is passing by, pleads for her love. But Sarojini rejects his request. Enraged at this, Viswamohan makes an attempt to overcome her physically. At that moment, Chandrakumar and Jayachandran arrive. Upon seeing Viswamohan trying to molest Sarojini, both of them jump at him and drive him away.

As it was an outdoor scene, many people who had heard about the cinema shoot came to the garden to watch. Rosy noticed that they were all looking at her in wonderment. Some of them were pointing fingers at her, whispering to each other and laughing. But Rosy ignored all that and began acting, giving her full attention to the instructions given by Daniel.

Now they had to shoot the scene where Viswamohan, who is enraged at her spurning his plea for love, tries to molest her. It was Johnson who played the role of Viswamohan. At first Rosy was a little hesitant to retort with harsh words to his pleas. But, as she had done yesterday while shooting the love scene with Daniel, when she reassured herself that this was only acting, she could perform her role well.

When they were shooting the scene where Viswamohan grabs her hand, she suddenly realized that she had got her period. *Oh God, I don't have with me the rags I usually keep for such occasions! If I don't apply some cloth padding now, the white mundu I am wearing will begin to show bloodstains!*

Her face went pale. In one instant, Rosy found herself totally thrown out of the role she was playing. Her eyes dilated in confusion.

Even when Johnson's grip tightened over her hand, there was no response from her. She stood passively without moving.

Daniel immediately realized that something had happened to Rosy. Till then, she was acting her role perfectly well. Something had gone wrong. Daniel asked Lalan to switch off the camera and came near her.

Johnson too had realized that something had happened with Rosy. Otherwise she wouldn't stand stupefied like this. Or was she alarmed at his grabbing her like that? But for an accomplished actress like Rosy, such things should not pose a problem.

'Rosy, what happened to you?' Daniel asked her anxiously. Rosy looked around her. Daniel, Johnson, Peter who was playing the role of Chandrakumar, Lalan, the assistants and crew of Daniel, the huge male crowd who had come to watch the shoot... Only men. Today Kamala and Reena were not there. And Janet had not yet arrived.

I am the only woman here. How can I tell anyone among them what has happened to me? But, if I stay like this for another moment, bloodstains will start spreading on my mundu. Oh God!

'Rosy, tell me, what happened?' Johnson's face was totally flustered

She didn't wait to answer that question. She lunged to the shed near the studio, in a movement that was between a walk and a run. Though she heard people calling her name, she ignored them.

Once inside the shed, she removed her mundu and examined her body. If she didn't get some cloth soon, the mundu provided by the studio would get spoiled. *Oh God, whom shall I tell about my woe?* She had never thought that this disaster would happen on a shooting day. This time, she also didn't have the body pain and stomach ache that usually preceded her periods.

Rosy removed her mundu and sat on the floor

She lost count as to how long she sat there like that. Suddenly, she heard an agitated voice from outside: 'Rosy, where are you?'

It was Janet's voice; it was coming towards her, along with the sound of footwear on the ground.

Rosy called out in a low voice, 'Madam, I am here.'

'Rosy, what happened to you? Everyone is scared. Daniel said you just ran away from the camera,' Janet said anxiously from outside the closed door

'Ayyo, Madam, that is...me...I have...' Due to

embarrassment and shame, words choked inside Rosy.

'What is it? Are you having stomach pain or something?'

'Madam, it is not that...'

'Ha! Tell me frankly, koche. Whatever it may be, you can tell me.'

Rosy fell silent for a moment. *If I can't tell this to Janet Madam, who else can I confide in here?*

'Chechi, I am having my periods. It happened all of a sudden. I don't have any cloth with me. If the white mundu gets stained with blood...how will I face all these people?'

'Ayyo, koche. Is that the matter? Okay, you wait here. I will get some cloth and another mundu for you,' Janet's footsteps receded.

Rosy sat there all huddled up. *Now, Janet Madam will go and tell Daniel about this. Then Johnson Sir will come to know of it. Chee! All of them will now know of this! What a shame!*

But anyway, Janet Madam has to inform Daniel Sir about this. In fact, what is so shameful about it? It happens to all the women in the world. It happens to Janet Madam too, month after month. Yet, on such occasions, women are put through so much embarrassment.

Very soon, Janet came with some padding cloth and a nice mundu for her to wear as a costume. After washing away the blood, Rosy changed her dress and went with Janet to the shooting site.

Daniel only looked at Rosy and gave her a smile. After that, he got busy with Lalan, preparing for the shoot. Johnson also just looked at Rosy and gave her a sweet smile.

But Rosy noticed that all the men in the crew, even while they were engaged in their work, were giving her curious looks. Rosy felt that all of them were giving sideways glances and winks as if they hadn't seen her before. On the lips of some people, she could also see a crooked smirk. *Somehow, they have all come to know what happened to me!*

But Rosy was not all that perturbed by this. Her mind was at peace. *What happened to me was something that happens to the wives and sisters of all present here. If my present condition brings cheap curiosity and vulgar smiles to their faces, it is not my problem. It is their problem. It only means that they don't yet know women, that's all.*

Janet, on the other hand, seemed to take special care of her during the rest of the day. For lunch, as promised the day before, Janet had brought mutton cutlet and fish fry. She took a special interest in making Rosy eat all of it.

'You have been suffering from the villain's molestations, isn't it? So, in order to recover from your weariness, you should eat well,' Daniel, who was strolling in the front yard after his lunch, said smilingly to Rosy.

EIGHT

THE NEXT MORNING, as Rosy was walking towards the studio with her lunch box in hand, she saw a huge crowd milling around VJT Hall. The whole place was decorated with flags and festoons.

Rosy slowed her pace. *Oh, these people are all from my own caste, the Pulayas,* she noted with astonishment. *How come a crowd of Pulayas have gathered here? Usually only the well-to-do people conduct meetings at VJT Hall.*

As she came near the hall, she peered closely at the crowd. She discovered that there were some familiar faces amongst them. There was Mathu Annan from Amathara, the man who was always busy working for the advancement of the Pulayas.

She had also heard that he was close to Ayyankali, their leader.

Mathu Annan was very close to her father when they were staying at Amathara. Those days, Mathu Annan used to come to their hut and urge her father to take part in the activities of the Sadhujana Paripalana Sanghom—Organization for the Welfare of Poor People. But her father always tried to evade him because, according to him, the Sadhujana Paripalana Sanghom people looked at newly-converted Christians like them with animosity. But now, people said there was a lot of change in their attitude towards them. Her father used to say that it had been a long time since they all joined LMS church; so now let them follow that path.

Mathu Annan was engaged in a serious discussion with someone. Rosy waited till they had finished their conversation. Then she approached him.

'Look who is here! Rosy?' he greeted her with joy. 'You came for the meeting?'

Rosy almost laughed. 'Oh, Anna, no!' She explained to him about her acting in cinema. After that, she asked why such a Pulaya crowd had gathered there.

Mathu answered her with great enthusiasm. Today, the anniversary celebrations of Sadhujana Paripalana

Sanghom, the largest organization of Pulayas in Travancore, were about to begin there. In the past few years, the annual meeting of the Sanghom had been conducted on the day after the conclusion of the Sreemoolam Praja Sabha conference. Today too was like that. Ayyankali was delivering the welcome address. Dewan V.S. Subramania Iyer would preside over the meeting. They were accompanied on the dais by high officials like the Chief Secretary and Peshkar. In other words, the Sanghom had grown into a force to reckon with, concluded Mathu excitedly.

Suddenly, as if he remembered something, Mathu told her, 'Rosy, don't you want to meet Ayyankali? He will be very happy to know that there is an artist like you from our community.'

Rosy felt embarrassed: 'Ayyo, Mathu Anna, why bother him? Who am I to meet such a great person? Moreover, why take such trouble especially when the meeting is about to begin—'

'Chee! There is no question in this of troubling and all that. You come with me. Let us go and meet Ayyankali.'

With Mathu Annan giving her such a command, Rosy had no other option but to follow him. She was meeting Ayyankali for the first time. He had a personality that stood out in any crowd. Though there were wrinkles and folds of age on his face, overshadowing it all was a strong sense of purpose that beamed through his eyes. Added to it was his elegant gait and the way he stood, all of which had a certain vigour and vibrancy. The shirt, coat and mundu he wore, along with the black-bordered white head cap, all added to his majesty.

He was standing there glancing through some papers he held in his hand. After inviting his attention with a cough, Mathu Annan said: 'Anna, this is Rosy. She is one among us. She is an artist. Now she is acting as the heroine in a film which is the first to be produced in our country.'

Ayyankali looked at her curiously, and at the end of it gave her a bright smile. Then he said, 'Koche, I haven't seen any film. They say it is a wonder. Anyway, it is good that you became a heroine in this new invention.' In response to his queries, she told him in her own way whatever little she knew of cinema.

'I have once said—I don't know whether you've heard it—that a time would come when there will be at least ten BA degree holders from our community. But I hadn't even dreamt that there would be a film actress from amongst us. You became a heroine without anyone telling you. I wish you all the best.'

Rosy folded her hands and lowered her head in respect and gratitude. Meanwhile someone approached Ayyankali to inform him about the arrival of Dewan, upon which he hurried towards the stage.

People from the Pulaya community were still crowding in and around the hall. There were a lot of women too among them. Rosy noted that their faces were brimming with a kind of excitement and enthusiasm that she had never seen when they were at their huts or in the workplaces.

She wished she could take part in the meeting, at least for some time. But she had to give up that desire as she would be late to the studio. Bidding farewell to Mathu Annan, she started walking towards Pattom. She walked briskly though she was tired due to menstruation and stomach ache. That she could meet a great leader like Ayyankali and receive his blessings also invigorated her, acting as a balm to overcome her physical fatigue.

Those of us who got converted to Christianity never had to face very severe abuses because of our Pulaya origins. As for me, I never had to seek anybody's permission to join the school or to study up to the third standard. I have heard about the oppression and humiliations faced until recently by those amongst us who remained in the Hindu fold...It was Ayyankali who fought against such oppression and won Pulayas their dignity as human beings. Father and Mother are not very fond of Ayyankali due to his caste status, but for the LMS people, he is definitely a great man.

Recently, I came to know through Mala that Ayyankali and his friends are organizing struggles to win permission for the Pulayas, who are also Hindus, to enter and pray at the temples. All the prominent Pulaya leaders are at the forefront of this struggle. Mala is yearning for that day when all Hindus are free to offer prayers at all temples. She always used to talk about a wish of hers: she wanted to enter Sri Padmanabhaswamy temple and offer prayers. She used to say her heart throbbed whenever she passed Puthenchantha street and saw that magnificent temple. Who knows whether my dear friend's wish will be realized?

If one could believe Mala's story, more than anyone, the Pulayas had the right to enter the temple. Long, long ago, the whole area was covered with dense forest. It was called Ananthankadu. There were also a lot of Pulaya huts there. One day, while a Pulaya woman was cutting weeds in the paddy field, she heard the cry of a baby. The cry came from the forest. She ran into the forest and found a boy child lying on the bare ground.

What a glorious child! Suddenly, a snake crawled towards him and spread its hood above the child's head as if to protect him. The Pulaya woman ran back to her husband to inform him. Soon, both of them came back to that place and, in a coconut shell, made an offering of flowers and fruits to the child. At that moment, the child disappeared. Upon hearing about the incident, the king of Venad decided that it was Lord Vishnu who had appeared as the holy child, and ordered that a big temple be made on that site. That was how the Sri Padmanabhaswamy temple was built.

But now the Pulayas could only tell such stories. Now if a Pulaya dared to go near the outer wall of the temple recounting such stories, one could imagine what would happen!

Though Rosy wanted to tell Kamala and Reena about her meeting with Ayyankali as soon as she reached the studio, she didn't have time to do it since everyone was busy with the shoot. She could share it with them only during lunchtime. But they didn't show as much excitement about Ayyankali as Rosy expected. They both seemed to be wondering what Ayyankali, his organization and struggle, had to do with their poor lives!

Only when she could share the news with Mala the very same evening did Rosy get over the disappointment she felt about the cold responses of Kamala and Reena. When Mala hugged her saying, 'Oh! You are really fortunate!' she felt the very same thrill as when she had talked to Ayyankali.

Once the next day's shooting was over, they arrived at that momentous occasion: the final day of the shoot! How quickly it had come! When Rosy, playing Sarojini the heroine, happens to see the mark on the shoulder of Chandrakumar, who is her lover's best friend, she comes to realize that he was actually her brother who was kidnapped by the robbers when they were children. This recognition happens towards the end of a big fight in the presence of Sarojini, when Jayachandran and Chandrakumar overpower the villains, Bhoothanathan and Viswamohan. Following this, Sarojini's parents are informed, and the film comes to an end when they are reunited with their dear son, whom they thought was lost forever.

The days of exciting hustle and bustle were coming to an end. No more would there be the glamour of cinema which had prevailed over them these last days. Everyone in the studio was aware of this from the morning, and an air of melancholy lingered over the studio. But Daniel had thought of something which could dispel this gloom to some extent at least. To mark the closing day of the shoot, a special feast was arranged. So, by noon, all the artists who had played any role in the film congregated at the studio. The feast was prepared in the studio premises itself, under the supervision of a pattar swami who was famous for preparing such feasts.

Rosy was partaking in such a feast for the first time in her life. Various curries, side dishes and different kinds of payasams followed one another. Though everything was good, she didn't find the dishes in the feast as tasty as the cutlet and fish fry that Janet had served a few days back. Rosy felt that the reason for that must be because the shoot was getting over that day. Though she had participated in only ten days, she felt as if she had been acting in films for a long time. She was completely engrossed in the world of film acting. Though there had been some hassles in between, the hubbub of the shoot, her heroine status, the presence of people like Daniel, Johnson, Janet, Kamala and Reena, the morning and evening walks seeing sights by the roadside—all this made the last few days very enjoyable. In another few hours everything was going to end. Again, Rosy was going to return to her beggarly life. In fact, even in that moment, she felt that all the recent cinema days were nothing but a dream.

Once the feast was over, there was a group photo session that included all the artists and crew of the film. Even during the shooting, all the important acting scenes were photographed, so that they would be preserved as 'stills' and not just in the reels of film. That included some scenes where Rosy too was present. It was the first time in her life that she was photographed, and she thought that later she should get one of those pictures for herself from Daniel.

Before evening, the shooting of the last scene was over, in which Chandrakumar, his parents and Sarojini were together, happy and laughing. Rosy had to struggle a bit to overcome the sorrow that filled her heart as the cameras whirred for the last time, and to bring the expression of a happy smile on her face. Yet, on that auspicious occasion, she managed to act to Daniel's satisfaction.

When Daniel announced that the shooting was finally over, everyone clapped loudly. In the green room for women, Rosy, Kamala and Reena took off the costumes and ornaments they had worn for the film. From now on, it was back to the dull and cheap dresses that they were used to. When Kamala took off her beautifully carved earrings, she sighed: 'It may be only for a wee bit, so let us wear it for that long. When are we going to get another such chance in life again?'

Though Rosy smiled without saying anything, sadness hardened within her too. She may have worn these glittery things only as part of her make-up, yet when she took them off, she felt a twinge inside her.

The only thing left was to receive the wages for one's work and leave the place. That was all.

Sitting in his office, Daniel himself was disbursing money to the prominent ones among them.

Forcing Rosy to sit in the chair in front of him, Daniel told her: 'Rosy, actually it was you who infused life back into my film. You must know about the troubles I had to undergo to find a heroine. In fact, I should pay you more than what I promised.'

Rosy's eyes glowed in happiness.

Pulling some notes from a wad that he withdrew from the table drawer, Daniel continued, 'But, koche, at present I am unable to pay you anything more. Cinema is a business that consumes money like fire. As of now, I am not in an enviable position. Your wages work out to fifty rupees, at the rate of five rupees per day. Now, I am paying you ten rupees extra. God willing, I will make a film again—in which case, you will definitely be in it. We will settle all dues then.'

Extending both her hands, Rosy accepted the money from him. Rising from her chair, she told him, 'Sir, please convey my regards to Janet Madam.'

'Definitely,' Daniel replied with a big smile.

Bowing low before him, Rosy moved towards the door. She stopped there, and with a shy smile on her face looked back at Daniel.

Daniel looked at her quizzically: 'What happened, Rosy?'

'Sir, I wanted to ask you something...' she faltered.

'Come on, go ahead.'

'Sir, I don't know the title of this film...' Rosy's eyes narrowed in bashfulness.

Daniel broke out in laughter. When it subsided, he said: 'This is not the heroine's fault. I should have told you earlier. The title is *Vigathakumaran*. Okay? In English, it is *The Lost Child*.'

When she came out of the room, laughter overcame Rosy too. *I am the heroine of the film. And so far I was acting my heart out in it without even knowing the title!*

While bidding farewell to everyone, Johnson said to her, 'Look, Rosy dear. In the future, when you become the heroine in other films, won't you give these poor guys a role in them? Please don't forget us.'

Chagrined, Rosy pursed her lips: 'Leave me alone, Sir. God will punish you if you mock poor people like us!'

When Rosy came out of the studio, Kamala and Reena too were with her. When they crossed the gates of the studio compound and stepped out on to the street, Rosy turned back and looked at the studio once again from the outside.

I don't have to come here any longer. Nor am I a heroine any more.

Watching Rosy looking back and the expression on her face, Kamala said, 'Penne, you will be back in films. Hasn't everyone loved your acting? But look, when you become a heroine again, you should remember me and her.'

Walking along for a while, chatting with them, they came to the junction where Kamala and Reena had to take the turn to the road leading to their homes. They all lived in Trivandrum, so, hoping that they'd meet again, they parted ways.

After walking a few steps alone, Rosy went behind a huge shady tree by the roadside. She took out the money she had tucked in the folds of her mundu and placed it on her palm. Sixty rupees in all!

One by one, she unfolded and examined each note with great care. She was looking at such a huge amount of money for the first time in her life. Even her father wouldn't have seen more than ten rupees at a time. As for her, she only got one, or one-and-a-half chakram at most, for working at the crops or by cutting and selling grass.

Out of this, forty rupees were Thiruvithancode currency and the rest were British rupees. She was seeing British rupees for the first time in her life. She could make out that it was the British rupee because it had the head of Emperor George on it. She had heard that the value of the British rupee was more than the Thiruvithancode rupee by about half a chakram. *In which case, the wage I got is worth more than sixty Thiruvithancode rupees.*

She looked around her with fear. *God! What if some rowdies see me here, a girl by the roadside, all alone and with so much money on her? Good that no one has seen me yet.* In a quick move, she put the money back safely in the fold of her mundu and fastened it tightly.

Then, wearing a beggarly look on her face, she walked ahead—so that no one could guess that she had so much money on her!

A laugh broke inside Rosy. Even though she had

finished acting in cinema, she was continuing to act. If in cinema she had played a noblewoman, here her role stood out much more, that was all!

As Rosy walked along, she gazed keenly at the roadside scenes. Bungalows where rich people lived, government buildings, madams wearing stylish skirts and blouses, and sayips with hats on their heads and sticks in hand, lazily engaged in their regal evening walks in the cool breeze. The rumble of the bells of horse carts and hand-drawn carts. There were many such fascinating sights.

From tomorrow onwards, I will not witness any such scenes. Maybe never again. Who knows? Maybe once the movie Vigathakumaran *is released, as everyone says, I will be in cinema again, and then all these things may come back to me...*

When the coal gas bus passed her by with its horn blaring, she looked upon it with yearning. *At this moment, I have enough money to buy a ticket to get into that bus! One day, I should travel in this bus with Appan and Ammachi from Trivandrum to Kollam.*

Are Pulayas and other lower castes allowed inside the bus? Who knows? As we are converts, it may not be a problem. In any case, I should travel in this bus some day...

NINE

THE NEXT DAY Rosy stayed at home. When Paulose and Kunji had gone to work, Mala came to her. She would not be satisfied, however many questions she asked or however much Rosy answered her. She wanted to know more and more news about shooting for the movie.

It was through Mala that the news spread, in the huts of the poor and the houses of the high-castes, about how a girl called Rosy had become the heroine of the new art form called cinema. Most of them did not know what cinema was. To them, it was Mala who explained with her own embellishments the news about Rosy's acting in cinema.

Gangadharan Pillai who ran the coffee shop was

the only person who had seen cinema. He was at Salem a long time back. Over there he had seen some Tamil and Hindi movies.

He said to Mala, who had come in with some firewood to his shop, 'You and your Rosy. Edi penne, cinema is not child's play as you think. The heroines in it are fair like the whites. Not silly Pulaya girls. She is simply making up tales.'

Mala flared up, 'Yes, yes. You are the one who knows all about cinema. Rosy is not one to tell tales. Ah, why talk? The movie will be out soon, won't it? Then we shall see.'

'Vo, vo. We shall see your Rosy doing the role of a servant in it.'

When Mala told Rosy about Pillai's scorn, Rosy became angry. 'Lass, why do you fight with others about my cinema?'

But Mala felt sad that she could not say much more to Pillai because of the pitiable state that she was in.

It was through Mala that Rosy came to know about the contempt that people in rich and high-caste houses showed when they heard about a Pulaya girl named Rosy acting as a heroine in the movies. A Pulaya girl as heroine—impossible! The mistresses remarked that she must be doing the role of some servant.

Mala was determined for the movie to come out soon and teach them a lesson. As for Rosy, she felt amused seeing Mala's resolution.

When they both went out to cut grass Mala would ask, 'Is it time for your movie to be out?'

Rosy did not know anything about it other than that she was the heroine. What work remained, what would happen—all this she did not know. She only had the faith that the enacted scenes could be seen on a white cloth stretched across a wall in the theatre.

Once when she saw Johnson on the way, she asked him when the movie would be out. It would take some more time, but when the date was finalized Rosy would be informed, he said.

'Will the movie come out without the heroine hearing about it?' Johnson asked her in his usual joking manner.

In the meantime, something else was happening.

When she went to work to nearby places, people were pointing at her and saying things, or looking closely at her as never before.

Some high-caste men who had before pretended to be defiled when they heard the name of a Pulaya now started to come to her saying that she was beautiful, and that if she went along with them obediently, they would give her presents. Rosy sent them all away. In truth, none of this hurt Rosy much. She had known for a long time, by seeing and experiencing many things while she went to work, that at least some of the men belonging to high castes were those who took advantage of poor women.

But something that happened when she went for Sunday service to the church really hurt Rosy. She understood that some of the neighbours who were on friendly terms with her family when they stayed at Amathara now stood with a grim look on their faces. Margaret Pathachi and Lucy were people who were distantly related to her. Though they were standing next to her for the service, they did not even turn around and smile.

These were the women who would otherwise always affectionately ask after her. They were not bothered if the service was going on or if the missionary was preaching. They wanted to know and also tell her all the news before the service got over. *But today they are not even looking at me or Amma.* Rosy could not understand what the matter was, however deeply she thought about it.

As soon as the service was over, Rosy approached Margaret Pathachi. She was called Margaret Pathachi because she was adept at getting babies delivered. Those who were close to her called her Pathachi.

'Why, Pathachi, do you all turn your faces away as if you were angry with me?' Rosy asked, taking hold of Pathachi's hand.

At first, Pathachi tried to slip away by saying it was nothing. But when Rosy made no move to let go of her, she gave her a piercing look and said, 'Heard that you acted in the movies. Edi, is this work that God would approve of? Is this meant for us Christians? Earlier you hurt your father and mother a lot by acting in dramas and Kakkarissi. Was that not enough, that you've now decided upon the cinema?'

Though anger boiled in her, Rosy swallowed it thinking that Pathachi was a woman much older than her. Without saying anything, she left the place in haste, taking along Kunji who was waiting for her.

Even then, she knew that Pathachi and the rest of the women were still continuing to say bad things about her.

TEN

AS THE DAYS went by, Rosy was overcome by boredom. *How long can one stay alone engaged in doing things like cutting grass and clearing the compound of weeds and shrubs?*

One morning, when she was about to leave home for work, Mala's Amma, Velutha, came and informed her that Mala was not feeling well and was bedridden. Rosy went across to Mala's hut. What her mother said was right—Mala was suffering from body pain. Yesterday when Mala's aunt visited them, she had gone out with her; and it seems they had eaten some delicacy. It must be due to that.

So, she had to go for work all alone. *What is the fun in work, if there is no one to chat with and talk to? But one cannot get along in life just having fun.*

Rosy looked around her. There was no one. Sivaraman Pillai, the supervisor, had gone somewhere in the morning after assigning today's work to each one. *Okay, let me sit and stretch my back for a while to relax somewhere.*

The household was by the riverside. It belonged to the tharavad called Melevila which belonged to Janardhanan Thampi Muthalali. Both she and Mala had come here to work several times before.

As it was by the side of the river, the soil was very fertile. But there was no other crop except for a few coconut trees, and they were full of nuts.

From there, one could see no other houses anywhere around. Many parts of the tharavad had forest-like vegetation.

To relax, Rosy leaned on the base trunk of a kadampu tree that stretched its branches towards the river. *How nice it is, sitting here dangling my legs in the water and feeling the cool breeze...*

A few bunches of flowers were dancing their way along the river; the flowing water was very clear. They were manimaruthu flowers. With a stick that was lying nearby, Rosy tried to draw the flowers towards her. Though she could get hold of them, in an afterthought she dropped the attempt. *Let them flow—let the manimaruthu flowers dance along the river in style!* Rosy waved towards the flower bunches and bid them farewell.

Even when she was last here, she had made special note of this kadampu tree. She had yearned to sit leaning her back against it and feeling the breeze. But Sivaraman Pillai or one of his assistants were always around the household. They never allowed anyone to sit idle for a second. Except for the brief lunch break when they had tapioca or kanji, they had to go on working during the rest of the time. Otherwise they had to listen to their stinking abuses.

Now is a good opportunity...One should have a house of one's own within a compound by the riverside like this. Then I could sit every day with my feet in the river. Maybe when I become a big film actress it will become possible. My wish might be fulfilled when I earn a lot of money by acting in several films.

But however big a film actress and converted Christian I may be, will the elites of Trivandrum sell their land to a Pulaya girl like me? Anyone among the elites selling their land to a Pulaya has been unheard of till now.

Yet my mind says that when I become a big film actress, after seeing me time and again, the elites will get to like me and their hatred and contempt that I am a Pulaya girl may disappear. Before the magic of art, the untouchability of caste will be dissolved.

But for all this to happen, films should get made here. And I should act in them too...

As of now, I feel the fact that I acted in a film seems to have happened a long time age.

She did mental calculations about it. *The film got over in the month of Medam—April–May. Now it is Chingam—August–September. So it has been more than three months now.*

But my film acting has become something that seems to have happened not three months but three years ago. Now there is no sign at all that I was once a film actress. This girl—whose whole body is sticky with sweat, hands and legs bruised by thorny shrubs, with sickle and spade in hand—this is the same girl who played the heroine in the film Vigathakumaran*? I myself am not able to believe it.*

'Aha, enjoying by yourself, is it?' Suddenly a rough voice from behind startled her.

Oh God, it is Sivaraman Pillai. I didn't even hear his footsteps.

'Penne, this is really nice. If there is no one to supervise for even a moment, you just skulk away, is it? Dangling her legs in the river, look at her sitting like a princess!'

Rosy got up, totally flustered. 'I was only...I was feeling tired, so...'

'If you try to play such tricks, you will learn a lesson or two from me,' Sivaraman Pillai spat out.

Rosy picked up her sickle and began walking towards the side where she was working. *There is no use explaining things to him.* Then he called her: 'Hey, stop there. Put your sickle down. I have some other work for you. Come with me.'

She didn't know what to do. *What other work is he going to ask me to do?* When she was following Sivaraman Pillai, he said: 'Edi, haven't you seen the coconut shed in the compound? You go and clean it. It's been ages since it has seen anything like a broom. If Thampi Sir happens to come here and wants to rest, there is no other place.'

Rosy had seen the coconut shed when she had come last time. It was situated in another corner of the compound. The shed was used to store coconuts. It had two rooms made of laterite blocks. She hadn't entered them till date.

When they reached the building, Pillai told her after spitting out the paan in his mouth: 'Look, the broom is here. Sweep and clean up the whole place. Tell me when you are finished with it.'

Rosy nodded in agreement and entered the building with the broom.

The room was full of dust and cobwebs. The moment she started using her broom, the dust rose in the air. Though it entered her nostrils and eyes, she went about cleaning the place with great care.

I should not let Sivaraman Pillai say that I am a slacker. I don't want to listen to his abuses again. It is not just the abuses, but I may not be called again for work if he gets offended.

There was a cot and two chairs in one of the rooms. *Maybe Thampi Sir rests here when he visits the place.* Rosy dusted the bedsheet and spread it on the cot neatly, then she heard the sound of footsteps outside the room. Before she could turn and look to see who it was, she heard a voice: 'You have cleaned the cot and the bedroom really well. I reached here at the right time, isn't it? Now I can straightaway lie down.'

There was Janardhanan Thampi, leaning on the door!

He was standing there with his head half-turned and a smile fixed on his face. Before this, Rosy had met him only once. At that time, he had been travelling along the road in a villu vandi. It was Mala who pointed out that it was Janardhanan Thampi. Even though he was sitting in the vehicle, Rosy was struck by the size of his body.

Now, when she watched him at close quarters, he looked double the size. His body was partially covered with a shawl, and the thick clutch of hair on his broad chest multiplied the wild vigour of that body.

Watching Rosy's panicked look, Thampi stroked his thick moustache, and laughed: 'Don't get scared—it's me, Janardhanan Thampi, the owner of this property.'

Rosy stood rooted to the ground. She was confused, not knowing what to say or do. It was the first time in her life that she was standing in front of such a big and important person. When one went for work, it was the supervisor who gave instructions and paid the wages.

Oh God, Pillai Annan never even gave a hint that Thampi Sir would come here now.

Thampi stepped into the room and said, 'Don't get upset. I don't observe untouchability and all that, especially with beautiful girls.'

Thampi laughed with his body shaking; his pot belly too shook and rocked along.

'Your name is Rosamma, isn't it?'

She nodded yes.

'Cinema actress Rosy. Haha, nice, really nice... Film actress Rosy has cleaned my bedroom. Great!'

Thampi slowly moved forward and sat on the cot. By then, Rosy was hurrying to get out of the room. She hesitantly asked him, 'I have finished cleaning the room. Shall I go?'

'No, don't go—stay here. I told you I don't observe untouchability or anything, especially with a beautiful film actress. I have heard a lot about your film affairs from others. But I never thought you were so beautiful.'

Rosy felt her face tightening.

'You come here,' Thampi gestured to a place beside him.

Rosy stood hesitantly.

'Edi, I asked you to come here.' Thampi's voice rushed at her like sharp knives.

Thampi got up from the cot. Then he looked at her face—it was a gaze that pierced its way to her innards. Then his inebriated stare travelled down over her body, lingering over the supple curves.

It happened in a split second. Thampi's strong arms caught hold of Rosy's body and tightened around it. Then, her body was thrown over the cot.

A shriek fluttered madly in Rosy's throat. Though for one moment she felt completely weak, in the next second she jumped up.

'No, no! Don't do anything to me,' she hissed.

With his left hand Thampi caught her right hand. Rosy was crushed by that tight wild grab.

Thampi told her in a voice brimming with lust, 'Rosamma, I like you very much. You don't have to worry. I will give you gold, money and land.'

'I don't want anything, Sir. I can't do this. I am not that kind of a woman.' Rosy's voice rattled.

'Edi penne, I know what these film actresses and theatre actresses are like. Don't think I don't know how cinema actresses in Pandiland and Bombay make their living. Only those who sleep around become actresses. I also know you slept with that Nadar boy Daniel who made the movie.'

Rosy said plaintively, 'No, Sir. No such thing has happened. Though I come from a poor house, I have never sold my honour.'

'Wow,' Thampi laughed contemptuously. 'As if all film actresses are paragons of virtue! Edi penne, stop playing tricks with me and come lie down here with me. You know how many princesses yearn to sleep with me? You come and give it a try, then you'll never regret it.'

Rosy was convinced that he was not going to leave her alone of his own accord. *He has lost his mind out of lust. If I have to escape from his clutches, I can't do it on my own. I have to pull a fast one on him.*

Suddenly Rosy looked at Thampi and smiled at him. She slowly brought her free left hand to his face and started caressing his rough stubble, tickling him gently.

Thampi looked at her in astonishment. A lustful smile spread on his face.

'Oh, so you know everything. You were just trying to work me up, isn't it?'

Rosy coquettishly moved her body and said in a titillating voice: 'Oh, if you pounce on someone like a tiger, who will not get scared? Come on, loosen your hold on my hand. My hand is about to break. You are so strong.'

Thampi gave an intoxicated smile, 'Ho, when you hiss like a leopard, how can I but grab you like this? Okay, I will let your hand go. Come here; let us lie on the cot.'

In the next moment, Rosy freed herself from Thampi's grip. Thinking that Rosy was fully heeding his wishes, Thampi's body relaxed. He leaned back on the cot in pleasure.

That one moment was enough for Rosy. She rose up and turned around in one swift movement. The next moment she sped outside the room.

'Hey, you whore, daughter-of-a-bitch...' Thampi shouted and tried to leap after her. But her pace was something beyond what his huge body could catch up with.

Rosy ran towards the riverside. Reaching the riverbed, she stood still for a second. The river was not very deep. She jumped in. Even in the middle of the river, the water level was only up to her hips. So, without much effort, she swam to the other shore.

Reaching the other side and taking shelter in the kaitha bush there, she looked back. On the other side Thampi was standing enraged. Pillai too was with him. Both of them were pointing at her and saying something.

Then, she tried to get out of the kaitha bush. Thorns bruised her face and limbs; the pricks were oozing blood. But Rosy didn't feel any pain at all. Her whole body was in the throes of escape. The urgency of escape liberated her from all other pain.

As she wriggled out of the kaitha bush, a vast coconut plantation came into her view. She ran again. After a few minutes, she reached a public street. A bullock cart was passing by. Nearby were a few shops; some people were also standing here and there.

Rosy stopped running. Taking a deep breath and letting it out, she began to walk slowly. But the breathlessness of the sprint still shadowed her body.

The wet mundu she wore and her body, dirty with mud and bruised all over, attracted the attention of many people. Pointing their fingers at her, some of them were saying things and laughing.

Though such movements reached Rosy's eyes, none of them penetrated into her mind. Her mind was numb—its only mission was to find a way to get her body back to the hut.

Rosy was not familiar with that street. Yet she didn't need to ask anyone about which direction to follow to get home. From the interiors of her mind, an unknown sense of direction guided her feet.

By noon, Rosy reached her hut. There was no one there. Luckily, there was also no one around in the neighbourhood to see the wretched state she was in.

As soon as she reached, Rosy lay down on the mattress for some time. Pangs of hunger began to gnaw at her. It was then that she remembered there was no food at home. The kanji and lunchbox that she had carried lay somewhere in Thampi's compound.

It was a lunchbox that I have had for a long time. Appan had brought it for me during my sister's marriage, along with a new mundu and blouse piece. Now it is impossible to retrieve it from that compound.

For the first time after Thampi's attempt to molest

her, Rosy cried. She was thinking of having to leave her favourite lunchbox helplessly there; about the powerlessness of a poor girl losing the little thing that was dear to her and being unable to do anything about it.

While playing the roles of Kakkalathi and Parvathi, how many times had she eliminated many a cruel and vicious man? In explosive orations that were capable of shaking the universe and with limitless powers to curse, how many times had she faced those male savages who paid no heed to the individuality of women and attacked them, thought of them as toys to appease their lust? But when one such occasion arose in her real life—she couldn't do anything but run away. *I have spontaneously cursed him in my mind. But what is going to happen to big men like Thampi, when the inner being of a poor girl like me is wounded and a curse escapes from her?*

When she felt ravenous, she drank some water. But she felt it only added to the hunger that was burning inside her.

ELEVEN

ROSY DIDN'T UTTER a word to Paulose or Kunji about the humiliating experience she had with Janardhanan Thampi. She shared it only with Mala, that too the next day. Mala had come to Rosy's place with some luvikkas as she knew Rosy loved them. The two of them were alone in the hut.

Mala had brought the luvikkas wrapped in a towel. 'Come on, get up Rosy...close your eyes and open your mouth,' she said with a naughty smile.

'Hm? What for?' asked Rosy, lazily lying on the mat.

'Oh, you film actress, you'll get up only if you know what it's for, is it?' Running her hands over Rosy's waist, Mala tickled her.

'Hey, take your hands off me. I am getting up,' Rosy yawned as she sat up straight and leaned against the mud wall.

'Now that's a good girl,' Mala said, sitting beside Rosy. 'Okay. Now close your eyes and open your mouth.'

Rosy obeyed. Mala unwrapped the towel and put two luvikkas into Rosy's mouth.

But Mala did not find the laughter and joy that she expected from Rosy, who opened her eyes but did not show any signs of happiness even though she was relishing the luvikkas in her mouth.

In astonishment Mala took Rosy's hand and asked her, 'Penne, why are you so dull? I put luvikkas into your mouth, not poison!'

After Rosy recounted the ugly experience she had the day before, Mala went numb.

Then the two friends came to a decision—not to tell anyone about this. There would be no use spreading it. People like them could not fight and win over people like Janardhanan Thampi. Moreover, if someone heard them slandering him, Rosy might get into trouble again. So the only way out was to keep quiet about the whole thing.

From the next day, Rosy started going for work on the field with Mala. One day when Rosy and

Mala were going to Andiyirakkam where some women were needed for work at a construction site, they came across Sivaraman Pillai. He was coming out of a hotel after an elaborate breakfast.

Upon seeing him, Rosy and Mala looked at each other. Then they started walking hurriedly as if they had not seen him.

'Hey, you two! Stop there,' clapping his hands, Sivaraman Pillai called after them. 'Edi, Rosamma, come here, I want to tell you something,' he glanced around and moved to the shade of a jackfruit tree on the roadside. Rosy looked at Mala askance.

Mala said softly, 'You better go. I will wait here.' When Rosy still hesitated, Mala gave her a gentle push on her shoulder.

When Rosy approached, Sivaraman Pillai gave her a crooked smile. Rosy didn't understand what he meant by that smile. She only knew it triggered a lot of anger within her.

'Edi penne, what a foolish thing you did that day. Do you know how many women vie with each other to share a bed with Thampi Sir? And here you come, playing chaste!'

He elaborately spat out the betel paan in his mouth and continued, 'Okay, leave it. Maybe you are not used to such things. It is okay. Thampi Sir is ready to pardon you. You made a mistake, that's all. If you say yes, I will take you to him. Don't know why, but it seems he has taken a liking to you. Otherwise, would he show such kindness? The rest depends on how smart you are.'

Rosy trembled all over; she felt scared that her body would be torn apart. Her face twitched. In the midst of that quivering, her mouth opened and the words came explosively out of her lips: 'Pfa!' Her eyes aflame, she said, 'Go and tell your master—if he wants such bitches, let him go and find them elsewhere!'

Rosy turned back and walked away. Stunned for a second, Sivaraman Pillai roared: 'You whore, you'll suffer for this. Everything of yours will be destroyed, you slut!'

Rosy reached where Mala was standing, and taking her hand she walked away briskly. Mala didn't ask anything, nor did Rosy say anything.

Yet Mala could make out what Rosy was feeling. Rosy's tight grip over Mala's hand said what was in her mind, even without employing any words.

The very next day, Rosy and Mala had to go to work in the compound of a house just next to Janardhanan Thampi's tharavad.

The moment they stepped into the compound, they heard a very rough voice saying, 'Who is that?'

Mala and Rosy were startled and looked towards the place from where the voice was coming. A middle-aged man was standing there, strong and well-built. *Must be the owner of the compound.*

'We came for work here. Chandra Annan told us that you need some persons to work in this compound,' Mala said in a faltering voice.

'Hm,' he snorted and looked at both of them from head to toe as if he was dissecting them. 'What are your names?'

Rosy was surprised. *What the hell is this? Enquiring about the names of the women who come for work is new.* She replied, 'I am Rosamma, she is Mala.'

Then he walked forward, and pointing his finger at Rosy, said: 'So you are that aruvanichi—that whore?'

Rosy and Mala were stunned. Something flared up inside Rosy.

'You slut, I know enough things about you. I don't have jobs for aruvanichis like you. We have enough female labourers here, they will do. Better not spread your stink here, so leave this place immediately.'

Rosy was standing rooted to the spot.

In a wavering voice, Mala asked, 'Ayyo, thampra,

what are you saying? What has Rosy done to deserve all this abuse...?'

He raised his hand, 'You shut up. I know the story of this slut Rosy—a hussy who claims to have acted in plays and cinema in order to lure handsome men into her trap. Hah! Trying to fool noblemen like Janardhanan Pillai, you dirty chool?'

Oh God! What all am I hearing? I tried to lure Janardhanan Pillai? So Thampi and Sivaraman Pillai have started spreading stinking canards about me. As for me, I haven't told anyone about it except Mala... But when they say it, I am a whore who goes around trying to seduce men!

He raised his voice again, 'Why are you staring? Get lost immediately.'

Rosy's eyes were brimming with tears as she said, 'Sir, whatever you have heard are fabricated stories. I have never tried to seduce anyone. But when Thampi Sir tried to molest me one day...'

She couldn't finish her sentence. Before that, he bellowed, 'Chee, get out of here. Coming to my place and abusing noble persons of our village? I will pluck your tongue out!'

Mala realized that it was dangerous if they stayed there for another minute. There was no use telling him anything.

Mala started walking away, forcibly pulling along Rosy, who was about to say something else. Then they heard from behind, 'Let that aruvanichi leave. What is your name? Mala, isn't it? You may work here if you want.'

Mala turned around and looked at him sharply. Then she spat on the ground, and holding Rosy's hand strode out of the compound.

After walking for a while on the street, Rosy suddenly stopped. Without looking at Mala's face, she said, 'Mala, why did you leave the job and come with me? He was angry at me. Why should you lose a day's wages because of me?'

Mala's eyes seemed to flare up for a moment. 'Edi, what did you say? That I should work in the compound of that scoundrel who abused you? What do you think of me? So I am like that for you...' Mala's voice wavered and the corners of her eyes became wet.

Rosy hugged her close and said, 'I said that out of pain. I said that when I saw you suffering on my account, isn't that true? Come, let us go. Anyway, jobs are not restricted to his compound. We will manage to get other jobs.'

But in the coming days, Rosy came to realize with a shock that Janardhanan Thampi and Sivaraman

Pillai together had polluted the surroundings. Even places where she had worked many times did not allow her to work any longer. From some places, she was driven out. The story was the same everywhere. On the pretext of being an actress, Rosy was trying to seduce upper-caste men. Rosy tried to lure Janardhanan Thampi when he was all alone in his bungalow. He in turn drove her out.

When she passed through the streets, Rosy began to realize many people by the roadside and in Gangadharan Pillai's coffee shop were pointing their fingers and mockingly laughing at her. She realized that many men were looking at her as they never did before, weighing and measuring her body. *For them, I am not the same old Rosy anymore. I am a whore roaming the streets to lure men!*

But more than all of this, it was something else that scared and pained her more: the thought that one day or another her Appan and Ammachi would come to know all these ugly rumours about her. The pain and humiliation they would suffer when they got to know of all this! She could already see it in her mind's eye.

Earlier, when the ruckus about her acting in Kakkarissi and plays happened, it had caused them considerable pain. Now, the situation was going to be even worse. In front of the local people, their dear daughter was being decorated with the honour of being a whore!

Most of the time, Rosy was scared to even look at their faces. Who knew when that question—tasting like the wind of allegation sweeping the land against her—would issue from their lips? She was rattled by the very thought.

As she was not getting any jobs in nearby places, she began going to slightly distant places like Andiyirakkam, Thirumala and Pangode. Though Mala could get jobs nearby, she insisted that she wouldn't go anywhere there, but instead would accompany Rosy to work in other places.

One day when Rosy was returning from the market after selling grass, Mala's mother Velutha was with her. Mala had gone to her aunt's house in Venganoor and would return only after a few days. Though Rosy enquired about many things, Velutha maintained an unpleasant demeanour. She didn't ask Rosy anything but kept on walking stiffly. After some time she said, 'Penne, people are saying a lot of things about you.'

Though she went pale for a moment, Rosy regained her composure and asked, 'What are they saying, Veluthaka?'

Velutha stared at her and said, 'Very bad things. I know you too have heard about them. Good for you if you take care.'

The next day Mala told Rosy that her mother had warned her not get too close to her. They all believed the dirty stories about Rosy. Though Mala had tried to argue with them, they were not convinced.

'Rosy, how can I live without your company? No, let people say or do whatever they want, I will be friends with you,' Mala said, sobbing like a child. 'I don't understand how my mother could believe such nonsense about you. Tomorrow, if people say such things about me, will she believe that too? Till now, you were like a daughter to her. And now...' She couldn't control her tears.

While she was trying to console Mala, a shudder passed through Rosy's mind. *Now it won't take much time before my Appachan and Ammachi come to know of this. Oh God...*Another shudder went through her whole body. *I should not waste another minute before telling Ammachi. She should come to know of this from me rather than from someone else.*

That night, since Paulose had informed them earlier that he would come home late, only Rosy and Kunji were there for their usual porridge dinner. After serving the porridge in two mud bowls, Rosy began to tell Kunji everything. From her lips issued a low voice in which she shared with Kunji everything right from Thampi's attack a few days back to the present humiliation and discrimination that she was facing from all quarters.

Even while she was telling Kunji everything, Rosy was worried how she would respond. *She may beat me or scold me...*

But even after she had told her all, there was no movement at all on the part of Kunji; only the trembling of her hands that held the braided jackfruit leaf, dipped in the pot that was almost three quarters filled with porridge.

It looked as if Kunji's eyes were travelling afar. She didn't even seem to be aware of Rosy's existence.

Rosy was worried. *Why is Ammachi sitting like a statue? It would have been better if she pounced at me and beat me. But this unmoving posture scares me.*

She shook Kunji by the shoulder and called her, 'Ammachi, Ammachi.'

Suddenly, Kunji woke up as if startled from deep sleep, and looked at Rosy. Her lips were unsteady. With a big sob, Kunji hugged Rosy and drew her close to her bosom. Then they both broke into a long wail.

After crying, Rosy felt a little better. Ammachi's

weeping seemed to take away her sorrow. Though Ammachi was deeply pained, Rosy suddenly felt much better in the sharing of a grief that only a mother and daughter can understand.

But they were not sure whether they should let Appachan too share this sorrow with them. In the end they came to the decision that for the time being they would not tell Paulose.

Next day, the news that Rosy had been waiting for arrived: a happy missive that was capable of dissolving all her sorrows.

The news was brought by a boy sent by Daniel. *Vigathakumaran* was going to be screened in front of the public, at the shed named Capitol which was not too far away from VJT Hall. It was the renowned advocate Malloor Govinda Pillai who would inaugurate the screening. The boy told her that Rosy and her family must be present for the screening.

Once the movie was out, maybe the very people who abused her now would come to realize Rosy's talents and congratulate her. For Rosy and her parents, this could be the beginning of good times. Paulose also shared Kunji's hopes about what Rosy had said while going to work in cinema. Moreover, Kunji was relieved that till now Paulose did not know about all the canards regarding Rosy.

Mala was the happiest among all. But she was also very sad that she wouldn't be able to attend the screening of the film. Her Ammachi had strictly warned her not to mix with Rosy.

'Anyway, something good is happening to you. It is okay if I am not able to see your cinema. Leave it. Even when you become a big personality, I will know that you were my friend,' Mala told Rosy whenever she met her without her mother's knowledge.

As the inauguration of the movie neared, Rosy's happiness also increased, but along with apprehensions. *Oh God, will people like that movie? How will I look in it? Though Daniel Sir said that my acting was good, will people like it when they watch it on screen?*

On the day before the inauguration, another major problem rose in front of her. *The inauguration will be a big function which several big people from the city will attend. Do I or Appan and Ammachi have decent dresses to wear for such an occasion? Maybe people won't take note of Appan and Ammachi. But what about me? If I go wearing an old blouse and mundu, won't they make fun of me?*

The only decent dress I have is the one I borrowed from Mala when I went to visit Daniel Sir for the first time. Though I tried to return it to her after that,

Mala didn't take it back. Let it remain with you, she had said, evading the issue. In a way, that was good. It is enough to save my honour now.

Then Rosy suddenly remembered one thing: she had not met Johnson for a long time. Usually, she used to meet him once in a while in nearby places. It was from Nani, who went to work in his house, that she came to know that some days ago he had gone to Madras for work. He would return only after some time.

So Johnson Sir won't be there for the inauguration. It was due to his kindness that I became a film heroine. Sad that he will not be there on the auspicious day...

TWELVE

THOUGH IN THE Thulam month rain fell the whole day, it stood aside for some time when evening came. As it had rained heavily, it was cool enough to soothe Rosy. She had to walk a long distance, but she would not sweat.

The family was walking from Thaikkad to Capitol Theatre. Kunji felt anxious even while walking. Though the heroine had entry for the movie, could the poor father and mother go for the programme? When she spoke her fears aloud, Rosy scolded her. 'Chee, what is wrong with you, Amma? No one will prevent us from entering. We are not nobody. Aren't we going there on Daniel Sir's invitation?'

Capitol Theatre was decorated. In front there

was a board on which was pasted the poster of *Vigathakumaran*. The faces of Daniel, Johnson and Rosy were on it.

It took a moment for Rosy to realize that it was her face. She stood stupefied in front of the poster. Along with her stood Paulose and Kunji.

'Is it enough for you to look at the poster? Are you not going inside?' Hearing Daniel's voice, she raised her head. Embarrassment spread in her eyes.

Daniel heartily welcomed Kunji and Paulose. By then, Janet and the kids joined them. Janet herself led Rosy and family into the theatre. Before she went in, Daniel informed Rosy: 'After the movie ends there is a small function where the main actors and technicians in the movie will be introduced to the audience. So you should come to the stage as soon as the screening is over, ketto.'

Rosy dreamily shook her head. *God, is this me who is experiencing all this?*

The theatre soon filled with eminent people. The ceremony was about to begin. After the welcome speech by Daniel, the inaugural speech by Malloor Govinda Pillai in all his oratorial splendour reached the audience.

Rosy and her family were seated at the corner, in the middle of the theatre. But knowing that many were taking notice of her, Rosy felt uneasy. She also felt happy.

Accompanied by the band, the red silk curtain rose proudly and slowly. The band ended their song. A moment. Then there was pin-drop silence in the theatre.

On the white screen, black letters became visible, first in English and then in Malayalam.

'Travancore National Pictures presents *The Lost Child—Vigathakumaran*.'

Loud applause broke out in the theatre, along with some shouts.

The names of the main actors and actresses were now being shown.

ROSY.

Though the name had appeared on the screen for a split second, she felt that it stayed on.

Suddenly she turned around to look at Paulose and Kunji. They were sitting wonderstruck. *Oh, neither of them knows how to read and write.* Rosy said slowly, 'Appa, it was my name that was written there a minute ago.'

The titles were getting over. The cinema was about to begin.

As the scenes were displayed, a man standing near the screen called out the context and dialogues in a thunderous voice.

Within seconds the audience was absorbed in the film. Rosy too became engrossed in it. She was seeing a movie for the first time. Forgetting herself, she entered the story of the cinema through the announcer's voice. She even forgot that she had acted in it.

Precisely because of that, when she first saw herself on the screen, she was stunned. *Ayyo, that is me—Rosy, big on the screen.*

Appan and Amma were saying something in wonder and glee. Paulose pressed his hand against hers.

Now the scenes in which Rosy appeared were coming one after the other. She shook off the surprise and started evaluating herself objectively. She closely observed her body language and the emotions on her face. When she felt that she had done well, she was happy. At the same time, she was worried when she felt she had done badly.

In the meantime, something else was taking place in the theatre. Whenever Rosy appeared on the screen, loud hooting was heard from the back. Though she did not feel anything unusual was happening at first, she slowly came to realize that someone was deliberately trying to make trouble. But who would come here and cause a ruckus?

Warning bells started ringing in Rosy's mind. It seemed like the shadow of something terrible, hitherto unthought of, was spreading all around.

She tried to shake off such thoughts and concentrate on the movie. Yet another beautiful scene now appeared. Sarojini was walking on the road and Jayachandran was taking the flower from her hair. Then followed their love-filled talk.

When Rosy started walking in the scene, pandemonium started. A roar rang out the moment Jayachandran took the flower off her hair and kissed it.

'Pha! Whore. What are you doing there, you slut? Stop it, damned cinema. Showing off your lust to respectable men after inviting them, are you?' Loud hooting, bad-mouthing. It was now rising from many sides of the theatre. Along with it began the pelting of stones at the screen.

Rosy felt that hell had been set loose in the theatre.

'If this is the case, you would even take off your dress and expose your cunt in the name of cinema! You are set off to molest this golden city of Ananthapadmabha, aren't you?'

'Don't let her go. That daughter of a whore is inside the theatre. We should catch hold of her!'

Shouts were raised along with the sounds of chairs being thrown away.

In a voice that trembled, Paulose said to Rosy, who was sitting still on the chair, 'Daughter, you must escape from here. Fast, fast.' Kunji also said the same thing to her. Without wasting a moment, she sped out of the theatre in the shade of the night, through the crowd.

By-lanes, public roads. When she felt that all her strength was draining from her, after running a long while, she stood gasping against a wall and looked around. *Oh, I have reached Vazhuthacaud.*

She stood listening silently for some time. *Are there any footsteps following me? No, nothing can be heard.*

It was dusk, and all was deserted. There were no horses or bullock carts or people walking by. Beyond the wall, she could hear the sound of two cats fighting.

Gasping, she began to move again.

Reaching home, she collapsed on the mat like a plant that had been cut at its roots. When Paulose and Kunji came a long time later, she was in a half-unconscious sleep. But they saw that even in sleep her body was shaking and her lips were mumbling something incoherent. Kunji sat on the mat stroking her forehead. Paulose sat on the stone at the corner of the front yard, staring out at the darkness. Though the hooting of an owl made him afraid, he felt that the owl was telling them something. He was relieved that in the night when there was no one with them, there was at least the owl to keep them company.

THIRTEEN

THOUGH MORNING LIGHT flooded into the hut when Rosy opened her eyes, not a drop of light entered her consciousness. It was a state in which she did not know who or where she was.

She lifted her body a little from the mat and rested against the mud wall. Pain, and the burning of wounds somewhere in her body. It felt like a heavy weight was placed on the muscles of her legs. She closed her eyes and put her head between her bent knees. She sat like that for some time; then recollection burst upon her like lightning. The premiere of the movie the evening before and the attack that had followed: every detail flooded her mind.

Everything had finished for her in an evening. The film actress called Rosy had ended in a matter of seconds. This poorest-of-the-poor Pulaya girl had thought that she could shine as a film actress! No. How could a Pulaya girl even have the courage to desire such a thing in a town crowded with rich and proud people? Unwittingly, her nails bit sharply into her palms.

All of a sudden, the flushed dawn dimmed, and darkness spread in the fiercely falling rain. Along with it came the gush of Rosy's tears. The tears that had collected from last evening now pushed themselves out stubbornly.

It seemed as if the rain would never stop—so also the heartrending cries that shook Rosy's body. Though Paulose and Kunji tried to comfort her by holding her close, it was of no use.

Then they left her to weep, thinking that it would comfort her. Instead they sat and looked at the rain. Paulose did not have to go to the white missionary's house as he was away on a long journey.

Paulose and Kunji did not have anything to say.

No, they did.

But they both read what had to be said from each other's faces.

The night before, Kunji had told Paulose about

all the indignities that Rosy had to suffer till then. Though she had feared that he would be angry with her for not telling him anything before, he did not react at all.

All he said was, 'Kunji, we thought we could make our daughter a grand woman by sending her to act, alle? We—no—*I* was a bit proud about that, I think. We did not think about how far a Pulaya girl was supposed to go. It is all my fault.'

Though it was noon, the fire was not lit in the oven. In the end Paulose himself skinned some tapioca, lit the fire and kept it on the mud stove to cook. Though they tried to force her to eat, Rosy could not swallow anything except a small piece.

After sleeping some more, when Rosy went to wash up, she heard a whisper from the fence at the side of the road.

'Shh...shhh...'

She looked towards it curiously.

'Rosy, this is me, Mala.'

She went in happiness and wonder. Mala had hidden herself behind a plant. Both friends looked at each other from either side of the hedge. Mala felt unhappiness breaking out when she saw the shattered state that Rosy was in. She knew about the disgrace Rosy had faced the night before and also about the attack in the theatre. With this, the filthy talk that was going on about Rosy had gained impetus. Mala's mother had forbidden her once more, in harsher terms, to be friends with Rosy. As her mother was at home, Mala had been waiting all morning for an opportunity to see Rosy without her mother's knowledge. When she saw Rosy coming out after her mother had gone, Mala ran over to see her. How much she had waited in glee to welcome Rosy after her first show—and how different their meeting now had turned out to be!

Mala cried.

Just then Mala's mother called out, 'Mala, edi, where are you?'

Mala pressed Rosy's hand from beyond the hedge and said in a voice filled with pain and anger, 'I am going, Rosy. I will try and see you somehow by dodging Amma's eyes.'

From the corner of her mundu she took a luvikka, and after placing it on Rose's palm she left hurriedly.

That night, Paulose, Kunji and Rosy had fallen asleep when stones started landing on the roof of their hut. Amidst loud yelling, they all woke up startled. At first the three of them did not comprehend anything. But in a matter of seconds they understood that a group of ruffians were deliberately attacking them. They also understood that they were sent by Janardhanan Thampi.

'The slut who tried to defame Thampi need not stay here. Slut's daughter, damn performer, we won't allow your loose morals here.' The name-calling went on.

Though the night grew long, the thugs stayed on and continued the pelting and the swearing. In the hut, three souls hid like mice in the hole. They were shaking, thinking that the gangsters would leave the road any time to enter their hut and attack them. If that happened, there was no one to counter or question them.

No one, no one to help us! Oh God, how much more should my poor father and mother bear because of me? Rosy sobbed in guilt.

When the ruffians had gone, Paulose and Kunji became afraid that they would come back and attack them more violently. Thus, despite the physical and mental strain which tried to push them into helpless sleep, they resisted with all their might.

Next morning, Rosy woke up hearing a rough voice asking if anybody was at home. Appan and Amma had fallen asleep some time early in the morning. Opening the door made of thatched palm leaves, Rosy looked out. Two policemen. Her heartbeat increased.

'Edi, is this the house of one called Rosy?' the policeman who was the elder of the two asked, looking at her from head to foot.

'Yes, Sir,' she said with a slight tremble.

'Mm, who is this Rosy?' he asked, settling his eyes on her rising and falling breasts.

'It is I, Sir.'

'So you are the one who created all this trouble, alle?' He twirled his moustache. By then Paulose and Kunji had woken up. They quaked upon seeing the police. 'Ayyo,' escaped from Kunji's mouth.

The policemen asked Paulose and Kunji some more questions, increasing their fear. Only after all that did they reveal why they had come.

As there was a chance of Rosy and her family being attacked, the policemen had been sent from their department on Daniel's request. The elder one was Pappu Pillai and the younger, Manian Pillai. 'What to say? When you sent your daughter for all this...you parents should have thought that trouble would be created,' Pappu said, after spitting out his betel juice.

The rest of the time they stood guard, the policemen treated Rosy, Paulose and Kunji as if they had done something wrong. 'What is the use of telling that we are first-class Nairs? It is our fate to stand guard in front of a Pulaya house. My Sreepappanava, this is Kali Yuga,' Rosy could hear them say on and off. Her tongue tickled with the urge to ask them to leave. But she controlled herself by thinking that the tongues of her people had been pawned as slaves a long time ago.

People from the street and beyond the fence looked curiously at the policemen in front of Paulose's house. She saw them pointing at her and saying things while laughing.

Even though the policemen had been sent by Daniel to guard them, Rosy felt that their presence outside the hut was degrading. She felt as though their looks were tearing her to pieces each time she went outside.

'She is a good one,' Pappu Pillai said as she was coming out of the bathroom. In reply Manian Pillai made an obscene gesture with his fingers and laughed.

However that night there was no attack. The next day Paulose and Kunji went out in search of work in the fields. As no one had gone to work for the past two days, there was nothing left in the hut to eat. The white missionary was not back from his visit to England and Paulose did not have his usual work at his kitchen. So he had to work for daily wages in the fields. Rosy told them to spend some of the money she had got for acting, which was kept in the earthen pot. But Paulose did not agree.

'No, girl, let it be there. That is not the money to buy tapioca and rice. Your mother and I will make the money to assuage our hunger by working outside.'

Rosy stayed inside the hut. Though she said that she would go in search of work too, Paulose refused, saying that it was not the right thing to do then.

Rosy felt suffocated just sitting and sleeping in the hut. If she went out of the hut for some fresh air, she had to bear the filthy talk and gestures of the policemen. The stuffy air and darkness of the hut was better than that.

Oh God, how long will I stay like this? The police will guard us for the next one or two days more. After that won't Thampi's people come searching for me again?

Once Rosy thought of telling the Ayyankali leader or Govindan Asan about her situation. But would an Ayyankali leader get involved in this problem? He was working for greater things, like the progress of the community. *Will it be possible to present my problem before him at a time when dirty stories are storming around me about my integrity? Are my problems the problems of the Pulaya community? I can't understand...*

About Govindan Asan. It is definitely possible to tell him about my problems. But what can Asan do? Asan cannot do anything against a lord like Janardhanan Thampi who rules over the land, or his followers. Not only that, Asan has suffered a lot for me during the time when there was that problem in Amathara. It is sad to trouble him again for me. No, there is nothing to think about here.

What if I go somewhere far away from this town? Far away in Madras or Salem where there is work to be done in movies and dramas. But one would have to try to find some job. And I do not have the money or the means to go there. If a woman goes alone to all these places, what will be the traps awaiting her?

God, if only some way could open up out of this hell! I don't want to be a queen or an actress. I just want to live in peace somewhere like an ordinary woman!

FOURTEEN

BUT ON THE same night, there was a change in her. Deep in sleep, Rosy was in the arena of dreams.

It was a vast ground. And the crowd was several times bigger than the usual gatherings for Kakkarissi plays.

The burning torches attached to the pillars exuded a mixed red and yellow light everywhere. On one corner of the stage were accompanists with their mridangam, ganjira and harmonium.

Rosy came on to the stage in the costume of Kurathi. The fingers of the accompanists began to press upon their instruments. Her recitation rose along with the crescendo of the music. Her legs gradually conjured dance steps.

Now, Shiva in the guise of Kurava was to come upon the stage from amidst the audience with a loud roar. Carrying a burning torch made by binding a cloth piece around a stick, it is an entry that creates ripples among the audience.

Since the time for the entry of Kurava was long past but he was not to be seen, Rosy slowed down her dance. Though her eyes searched among the audience for Kurava, she couldn't find any movement anywhere. She strategically began to repeat her song-and-dance all over again. Usually such delays never occurred. Who knew what had happened? She felt weariness all over her body.

When she took another step and pirouetted, she saw some movement among the audience. What first struck her were the lit torches. Not one, but hundreds of torches.

But none of the torches were in the hands of Kurava. They were held by monsters with huge bodies and cruel faces. Pushing aside the roaring crowd, they were rushing towards the stage. In the hands of each, the torches flared madly.

Rosy stood rooted to the ground. Her body seemed to have grown numb.

She desperately looked around for her Kurava. But he was not be seen anywhere. The monsters had already jumped onto the platform. The torches in their hands leapt dangerously towards her. She opened her mouth to scream loudly. In the same instant, she also opened her eyes. It took another moment for Rosy to realize that she had been dreaming.

Her body was drenched in sweat. But she felt relieved at having escaped from the terrible experience she was going through a few minutes back. She stretched her back and lay down. The same moment she was something startled, and she began shouting: 'Ayyo, fire, fire!'

The palm leaf-thatched roof and doors of the hut were all aflame. From outside were heard shouts, 'Burn it down!' 'Burn them to death!'

By that time Paulose and Kunji had also woken up. Kunji screamed loudly as she took the pot of water kept in the corner and poured it onto the billowing fire that was growing every minute. Paulose by that time had regained his composure; he grabbed both Kunji and Rosy and pushed them through the flaming door. Then he too jumped out.

When they got out, they could still hear shouts from the street. 'All of them have jumped out. Don't let her, that aruvanichi, get away! Catch her!'

Even in that pitch dark, Rosy saw them—in the street like a fort stood a group of toughies with sticks in their hands. *But where are the two policemen on guard? They can't be seen anywhere. Are they also with these attackers, assisting them in torching my hut and trying to hurt me? I don't understand anything!*

The assailants crossed the road and came towards them. Rosy stood aghast.

Paulose didn't wait any more. He took Rosy's hand and ran, dragging her behind the hut. As he ran, he said, 'Koche, you better run and escape from here. Me and your Ammachi will stay behind. It is you they want; they won't do anything to us.'

Anguished, Rosy said, 'Ayyo, how can I escape alone, leaving you both behind?' By that time, Paulose and Rosy heard the voices of the assailants coming towards them from around the hut. Paulose—not raising his voice, yet with the power of a roar—told her with his face just next to her ear: 'Edi, come on, escape. Run!'

Rosy nodded once and then, gathering all her strength, started running. Her legs flew above fences and ridges. She could sense that the assailants were following her, still shouting. After running through the narrow lanes for some time she reached the main road at Thycaud.

Rosy realized that it was dangerous to run through that wide-open road. If she ran like that, the assailants would easily catch up with her. But no narrow lanes were visible into which she could disappear.

Rosy strode forward rapidly towards a big turning. When she reached it, she heard a strange noise. She knew it was the sound of some motor vehicle.

Now the yellow glare of that vehicle was approaching the bend. The next moment, it reached the bend, ripping apart the veil of darkness.

It was a lorry!

Some thoughts passed through Rosy's mind like a whirlwind. Raising both hands, she ran towards the lorry and stood in front of it. With a terrifying noise, the lorry screeched to a halt just in front of her. Once her eyes got used to the blinding light, she peered inside.

Behind the steering wheel was one man with a turban on his head; on his left was another man, and behind them was a curtain covering some goods.

Rosy had heard that the one who runs the vehicle is called Driver. Going near and joining her palms before him, she cried, 'Driver Anna, please save me. Don't let them murder me!'

Driver carefully looked at her from head to foot and asked her in a loud voice, 'Who is this in the middle of the night? What is it?'

'Ayyo, Anna, I will tell you everything. But first please let me into the vehicle so that we can go. Otherwise they will kill me.'

The driver was about to ask her something else when terrifying shouts were heard on the road. Driver and Rosy looked in that direction. It was them. The assailants were rushing towards them.

Driver looked at Rosy closely once again, and then told her, 'Edi, get into the vehicle from the other side.'

Rosy ran across the front of the lorry and clambered on from the left side. The other man moved back to make room for her.

Driver took the lorry forward with a loud roar. Within minutes they sped past the group of shouting assailants who were running towards them, scattering them to the two sides of the road.

Soon they had crossed the town territory and were sure that the assailants wouldn't be able to catch up with them. Yet Rosy was still shivering. Needles of cold wind were piercing her body.

Though she had managed to escape from Thampi's henchmen, she was worried about the kind of persons she had sought refuge with. In the film she had acted in, it was easy to recognize the villains and the heroes. *But here, when I am fleeing with my life in my hands, I don't have any clue about my saviours.*

Rosy glanced covertly towards the driver on her right. As he had a turban on his head and there was not enough light, she could not clearly see his face nor make out the expression on it. She only knew that he was still young in age. It seemed the one accompanying him was a bit older. Though he had bruise marks on his face, he looked harmless. Once in a while, he glanced at her. Once, when she felt that he had given her a smile, she too returned a pale smile.

'Now, penne, what is your problem?' She was startled by the driver's query.

Rosy was confused about what she should tell them. *Should I reveal everything? But if they come to know that I am a cinema actress, won't they too think that I am a bad woman?* She had heard that those who work in vehicles are usually bullies. *And above all that, if they come to know that I am an actress, what will follow?*

'Mm, what is it? Why are you not answering my question?' Driver's voice had become a little gruff. *He is right; I should give an answer.*

Rosy began to talk. She left out details like being a Pulaya girl and an actress. Instead, she said her Appan had died when she was young; the history of the travails of her family consisting only of herself and her mother; the attempts of the nearby landlord to ruin her honour, his threats, attacks, and the attempt by his henchmen to torch their hut at night; and upon Amma's insistence, her desperate bid at running away from the town to escape from them etc. While uttering each word, she was mortally worried whether they would believe her words, or think that a dishonourable girl was making up a cock-and-bull story.

While listening to her tragic story, though the other man exclaimed, 'Ayyo!' 'Terrible' and other things once in a while, the driver didn't utter a word, except for some occasional grunts.

And it was from the other man that she gathered some information about them. The Driver's name was Kesava Pillai; the other one was Velappan. They were driving the goods lorry of Pioneer Company. Now, they were going to Salem with goods. Pioneer was the only lorry company in Trivandrum.

When they reached Nagercoil town, the lorry came to a halt in front of a small building that looked like a house. In front of the house were parked two or three lorries; there were a few bullock- and horse-carts, and some men associated with them.

There was a coffee shop that was open till late into the night, adjoining a house.

Kesava Pillai invited Rosy to the coffee shop. While they were sipping ginger coffee sitting on a bench, she could feel the gaze of many of the vehicle men on her. She was sitting alone on a bench. Kesava Pillai was talking to some of the lorry drivers.

After finishing the coffee, he asked her, 'So, where do you want to go now?'

From the light of the hurricane lamp that hung from the roof of the coffee shop, she now saw him clearly. Kesava Pillai was standing right below the lamp.

At the most, he was thirty years old. Though he was not very handsome, the tranquillity that his face and body exuded proclaimed a certain strength.

Rosy rose up from the bench and said, 'Anna, I can go anywhere except my hometown where I have lived till now.'

Kesava Pillai took off the turban and wound it over his head again. Then he asked her: 'Would you like to come to my house? Only my mother stays there. My house is just beyond this town.'

'Your wife and kids?'

Now, for the first time since they met, Kesava Pillai laughed—revealing the stump of a half-broken tooth in his mouth.

'But I haven't yet married.'

Inadvertently, shyness spread over Rosy's face.

'Then are you coming with me or not...?' he asked her seriously again.

Rosy was perturbed. *This is a crucial moment in my life—a call to another life that departs from mine till now. What awaits me there? Is it good or bad? Don't know...*

But I know one thing. The one who is calling me now saved my life. Whatever it may be for, I don't have any other call in front of me now.

Rosy nodded in agreement. Though Kesava Pillai's face continued to look harsh, she felt that she detected a smile in his eyes.

When they were stepping out of the coffee shop, Kesava Pillai said, 'Edi penne, at this time of the night I am not taking you to my house. We will go directly to Salem now. When we return from there after two days, I will take you to my mother during daytime.'

Again the lorry continued its journey through the night, traversing terrains unknown to Rosy. Even though the cold wind struck her face, she didn't shiver. She felt that her body and mind had reached a comfortable warmth.

But her mind gasped at the thought of Appan and Ammachi, and what they would be doing now. *Would Thampi's henchmen have hurt them, or completely burned down their hut? Will I see my Appan and Ammachi again in my life? Have I lost my sister and brother and all of them forever?*

She was suddenly perturbed at remembering something—the money in her cashbox! All the money that Daniel Sir had given her for acting in the film was in that box. It was the wealth that Appan exclusively kept for his daughter, without spending a chillikaash from it even in the face of the severe difficulties they had had at home in the last days. It contained not just money, but all the love that Appan had for her...

Has the fire that devoured the whole hut burned to ashes that box too?

Though she tried to control her sighs, when the figures of her Appan and Amma appeared in her mind, she burst out into sobs. Velappan Pillai looked at her with sympathy. Then he whispered something into Kesava Pillai's ears. But Kesava Pillai, after giving her a sideways glance, went back to concentrating his attention on driving.

As if he knew she has to—and will have to—cry like this, now and many times later.

FIFTEEN

IT IS A silence in which you cannot hear even a leaf moving. The people, the cattle, the houses and streets are all sleeping in the scorching heat of the summer where even running water will slumber.

Daniel Sir, Janet Madam and the children are all asleep. It will take an hour more for all of them to wake up and drink their evening tea. Then it will be fun with lots of shouts and laughter and song and dance.

Though it is nice to watch all that, it is a game in which my life is at stake. If the eldest, Sundaram, or the youngest, Haris, are having a fight or if the fight is between Haris and his elder sisters Sulochana, Lalitha or Vijayam, it is my life that becomes their toy. My life shortens as the children tear apart or burn down their toys.

Looking at it that way, it is better that the children are asleep. Curled up in a deserted corner of the long veranda lined with wooden railings, I am startled each time I hear their footsteps. I know that my days are numbered.

Oh! You did not understand who I am? Rosy—yes, I am Rosy.

I am now staying in a house in Madurai. A fairly big house that is neat and clean. For the past ten years I have been living in this house along with Daniel Sir and family. You are confused, aren't you? You can't understand, can you, how I who had escaped with my life with Kesava Pillai in a lorry is now staying along with Daniel Sir in his house?

I am not her who went along with Kesava Pillai in his lorry. She who went that day is not Rosy now. That night itself she ceased to be Rosy. From then cinema and drama completely drained away from her and she became Rajammal. Rosy who found her saviour in the lorry driver Kesava Pillai now lives in Nagercoil as his wife.

There have been troubles and tears in life even after that. Though she got a loving husband in Kesava Pillai, some days she dreams of a film actress called

Rosy. A Rosy living like a queen after becoming everyone's favourite since she acted in a movie called Vigathakumaran. *She cries silently without her husband and children hearing her when she gets up from the dream.*

But the times when Rajammal cries for the film actress called Rosy is decreasing. In a way that is best for her peaceful life. Let the poor housewife called Rajammal forget Rosy completely. Never dream about Rosy. Let not the bounds of her heart's peace be shattered by the lashing waves of Rosy's memory.

Now, about me.

Rosy. The girl who lives as Sarojini, whom Rosy gave life to, in the movie called Vigathakumaran. *The girl who lives in the reels of the cinema called* Vigathakumaran *that lies drowsily in the green painted square box placed in a corner of this veranda.*

This is the only print that is left of the cinema which once meant everything for Daniel Sir. The children have destroyed nearly half of it. It was mostly destroyed by Haris, the naughtiest of the lot.

Now Haris, who is nine years old, often fights with his brother Sundaram who is elder to him by ten years. Do you know how the younger brother lets off his anger towards the elder one? Haris cuts off those scenes of the film in which Sundaram acted as a four-year-old. Then he sets fire to them. Now not one scene remains of the parts which Sundaram had acted in.

Now and then, Haris and his sisters play a game. This is how it is: They take out the print of the film and cut off parts from it. Then they set fire to it. The children say that it is nice to see the celluloid burning in bright blue flames. How many of my life's scenes have thus dissolved into bright blue colour in the air?

The children have yet another game. They fold and unfold the reels at great speed. When you do that, you hear a flapping sound. They like this game very much too, in which the reels break apart.

Haris has another hobby too. His favourite actor is a Tamil film actor called P.U. Chinnappa. Chinnappa's fight scenes are dear to him. His greatest desire is to fight on the horse with the sword, defeating his enemies like Chinnappa does. He watches all the new Chinnappa films along with his family, holding his breath.

Just near his house lives a Tamil boy called Nagarajan, Haris' best friend. His father is the representative of some theatre company. So Nagarajan gets the tattered prints of movies from his father. These may also contain remains of Chinnappa's movies.

Haris and Nagarajan have a business arrangement. When Haris gives him some prints of Vigathakumaran, *Nagarajan gives him some Chinnappa prints in return. Thus, tearing up* Vigathakumaran, *Haris has stocked up a lot of Chinnappa film rolls. Opening these rolls, he would feel bliss looking at Chinnappa's performances. How many scenes of mine have reached Nagarajan's hand by now for Chinnappa's sake? None of them are left. They have all been destroyed by sunlight and moisture.*

You may ask if Daniel Sir does not see these agonizing scenes. He does and does not. Daniel Sir... He is the one who created me. Today he is just a shadow of himself. This is not the same Daniel Sir whom I had seen first with wild strength roaring in his muscles made strong by exercise, eyes sparkling with uncountable dreams. That courageous man who introduced the magical world of cinema to the land of Malayalam is now no more. The one who is left is an unfortunate man who gave a lot of energy and money for that wonderland called cinema, and who had to tear away from his own land to this foreign one, bearing the brunt of everybody's ridicule.

Yet this man dreams, now and then, like Rajammal. His dreams are about him who has become the favourite of this land as he produces movies that run 'Houseful' in all the theatres across the land. But these dreams do not bear the glitter they had in his youth. Now his dreams are filled with the scorching yellow light of impossibilities and disappointments.

Daniel Sir now has possibilities of a good livelihood, since he studied dentistry to get out of the financial crisis he had fallen into after his cinema production. He is in a position to own a good house and car, and give a good education to his children.

But even while leading this secure life, at the bottom of his mind lies the soreness of not becoming a film person—the illusion that someday he might be able to make a film again. Even while using tongs in the mouths of his patients for a livelihood, his hands are pining for a movie camera. To his eyes that swing between the struggle for existence and the memories and expectations of the tinsel world, these rolls of film do not make any impression. For him this square box with the rolls of film is as meaningless a sight as a stone lying on the ground or a weed at the roadside. I even doubt if his mind has accepted that we are toys for the children to play with.

Nowadays, a picture of Daniel Sir that I like appears to me sometimes. On some evenings when there is not much to do, Sir calls Janet Madam to his side. Beyond this veranda lies a small ground filled with tamarind and neem trees. Near them Daniel Sir and Madam would pull out two chairs and sit. Then he would ask Madam to sing some songs. When her songs—she can sing sweetly—rose into the air, he would sit silently and forget everything. Then his eyes would resemble the eyes of a young man. Eyes lit up with intoxicating love for his woman, eyes in which colourful dreams of films flutter.

There is a song that he makes Madam sing over and over again; the song specially written and tuned by Madam's father Joyalsingh for their wedding:

Let prosperity thrive forever
Let it prosper through good words
Beauty, joy and prosperity
Let all be bestowed on you forever
The deep love that emanates
From the primeval human being
One that obliges you like a slave—
Let it shine in you forever...

When he hears that song, tears of happiness or sorrow well up in the corners of Daniel Sir's eyes. I like to hear that song.

Oh, the house is slowly waking up from afternoon

slumber. Sounds from the kitchen, of Janet Madam using the vessels. Must be preparing tea. It is after they have had tea and the snacks their mother prepares for them that the children go out to play.

Will they come here to play today or not? Did not hear Haris today at all. Usually his voice rings out loudly by now. Has he not woken up till now?

After some time I get to know that Haris is down with fever. Janet says that his body is burning hot. He is lying tired in his cot. Daniel Sir is giving him some medicine.

Suddenly a wind of comfort blows through me. As long as Haris is lying sick in his cot, I am safe. It is when he is there that the kids play more with the films. As he has grown up, Sundaram does not join in these games any more. Did I pray that Haris would be sick for long?

Lord, let me not have sinful thoughts. Though my life is at stake due to his naughtiness, let nothing happen to him. Poor child. He does not know what he is doing.

It is the same creator that made me and him. But it is doubtful whether even a faint form of mine is there in my creator's heart. Now his five children are Daniel Sir's hope for the future. Haris and four other kids. Should I not pray that only good comes for them?

Though night has knocked on the doors of the house, I am lying awake. Except me, I think that all the others in the reel are asleep. Not many are left. Those who are left are Daniel Sir, Johnson Sir, Chellappan who acted as Chandrakumar and Wilson Singh who acted as the hotel manager. Kamala and Reena are now no more. How many more days for me?

Two glow-worms come and sit on the box. I look at them with interest. They do not fly away even after an hour or more goes by. They shed their blue light just near me. I feel happy seeing them shedding their light.

Some time later, without my being aware of it, sleep comes and covers me. Haris' fever lasts a week. All these days no one came near the square box.

After two days he takes a bath; even when his fever has subsided, Haris does not come near us. He plays other games with his sisters. I feel that he has completely forgotten about the square box and the rolls of film in it—he does not even look this side even after many days pass by. It is like that when children grow up. They will suddenly relinquish certain things or games they were interested in for a long time. Things they abandon without even realizing. When I was six or seven years old, I had a toy made from a coconut shell, in the shape of a monkey. That monkey was my companion when I woke and slept. But when I was bedridden with fever and woke up the next day, I never touched it again. It was much later, when I saw him among the spinach vines behind my house, that I even remembered him again.

SIXTEEN

BUT THE CHILD had not forgotten the toy inside the square box. When a cool wind was blowing at dusk on a particularly hot day, we were resting in a lethargy that was nice because it was rid of thoughts.

Suddenly I woke up when I heard Haris's voice quite near me.

'Ha, how many days has it been since we played with the film? Lalitha, you go and get a matchbox from the kitchen.'

Before he had even completed his sentence, Lalitha had run into the kitchen. *I was stunned; the danger which I thought was past had struck me again.* Then Lalitha's voice rang from the kitchen. 'There are no matches.'

'Oh, it is these children who finish off the matches so fast by playing with them,' the old cook scolded. 'That matchbox was bought two days ago and it got over so soon,' she grumbles.

Lalitha and Vijaya have left for the nearby store to buy the matchbox. Haris is standing here.

God, will I fall into his grasp today too? Which will be the reels the little hand will catch hold of this day? I run my eyes all around me. A tremble pierces me like a bolt of lightning.

I exist in just one more celluloid reel. The scene in which Jayachandran removes the flower from my hair and kisses it. Just one scene. In this world, I live only in this.

I realize this truth only now. Till now I had not thought about it. Though I knew that my life would come to an end in one of these children's games, I did not know that my life remained in this one reel. I search unbelievingly. No, nothing remains. If this reaches the child's hands—approaching the square box...

Nothing more to think about. I'm trying to shut out my heart. But I cannot. Will anyone be able to do it when life and death hangs on the scales of a balance?

'Harry, here is the matchbox,' Lalitha and Vijaya reach the veranda.

Now I felt a numbness covering me. It is a blessing considering the fact that any minute now Haris' hands will reach out into the square box.

The child's hands lower into the box. Though they search two or three times they do not reach the place where I am. But in the next search, it happens. I am there in one of the reels that are picked up.

Though Lalitha and Vijaya said that they could play the burning game in the veranda itself, Haris says that they should burn the reel outside. In all these games, his was the last word.

I am taken by them to the ground near the field of trees. Daniel Sir and Madam are sitting beside each other on cane chairs. Daniel Sir's body and soul are opened to a Christian Tamil song being sung by Madam.

The tender hands of Haris are touching me. In the softness of his fingers throbs the innocence of the world. But these very same fingers are going to put an end to my life. These innocent movements are rushing me towards great danger.

'This young girl, she is going to do great things in this land. She will do things that no one has ever done before, that will bring her glory.'

The words uttered by Kakkalathi when she came to the Amathara house when I was eight years old.

The words that Amma and I had forgotten. I still remember what she had said. It must have been upon seeing the scorn in Amma's eyes, that Kakkalathi said again, 'This is not a lie, Amma. It is the truth. A time will come when this child will make this family and Malayala Nadu proud.'

I remember her red nose ring and dark green saree as if I had seen it yesterday.

Is this the fortune that Kakkalathi talked about? My life that is going to be burnt down by a matchstick in the hands of this little boy? Will anybody remember that a girl like me was born on this earth and lived here for some years? Did I gain some glory during the time that I lived this life? Was it a thing of fame to act in the Kakkarissi or in the cinema? Did not acting lead my life to tragedy? It is Vijaya who lights the fire by taking a matchstick from the box. A flame jumps with greed into the reel in Haris' hand. The flame starts spreading from one corner to my side.

Let prosperity thrive forever
Let it prosper through good words
Beauty, joy and prosperity
Let all be bestowed on you forever...

The song that slowly rises into hopes of the bright new life that Daniel Sir and Janet Madam lead...God is letting me hear it again.

But Daniel Sir, who is engrossed in the song, does not know that the life of the girl whom he had lovingly nurtured is coming to an end. My creator who has the power to save my life does not know anything. I too cannot raise my voice.

I plead with Daniel Sir with my eyes. But he is unable to see it. The corners of my eyes throb with the heaviness of tears.

Haris' hands throw the reel away as it catches fire. The children roar with laughter. In the first twist of the reel, I feel the flames licking me.

But I cannot feel the heat of the flames. All that I can see now is cool flowing water. Water like I had seen flowing by the house of Janardhanan Thampi on the banks of that river; the flowers of manimaruthu that were flowing coyly on the stream of waves, that had given peace to the heart. The flowers brushing past my feet that are dangling from the river bank. Peace fills me from head to foot.

A miracle happens. The flames cannot destroy the flower on my head. It is safe in Daniel Sir's hands where he had picked it up to kiss it. Even as my body is being burnt to ashes, the flower is saved from being destroyed. The piece of reel with the flower falls at Daniel Sir's feet, flying in the breeze.

Though there were no roses in the vicinity, the sweet smell of roses emerged then. Daniel and Janet looked at each other in wonder.

AFTERWORD

Evening of 7 February 2006 at the Theatre in Gorky Bhavan Cultural Centre near Vanross Junction, Thiruvananthapuram

THE THEATRE IS packed with the audience who has been invited for the first public show of the documentary based on J.C. Daniel, directed by R. Gopalakrishnan and called *The Lost Life*. Haris Daniel, who lives a retired life in Salem, is on stage to share the memories he has of his father.

In the course of his speech, in a voice trembling with emotion, Haris said, 'These hands, it was with these hands that I nearly destroyed the whole of the first movie made in Malayalam land.'

Haris's words poured into the audience the pain and the heaviness in his heart. It was this man who destroyed the first movie of our land in a way that it can never be regained.

But in their hearts they said—wasn't it the prank of an innocent little boy? Whatever happened was only play which any child would indulge in.

But what had happened in that play! Sighing, they sat looking at him.

At that moment Haris looked around him in wonder. *From where is the smell of roses surrounding me? Ha, never till now have I experienced such a fragrance as this. From where is this sweet smell coming into the closed auditorium?*

Though he did not recognize that it was the smell of noble history, he thought that the fragrance was giving him a freshness and energy never felt before. Savouring the coolness, Haris continued his innocent words.

AUTHOR'S NOTE

P.K. Rosy

After being rescued by the lorry driver Kesava Pillai from the attacking mob, Rosy lived in Nagercoil in south Tamil Nadu till her death. After her marriage, she changed her name to Rajammal, befitting the tradition of her upper-caste husband Kesava Pillai. They had five children. Among these, the first three died. Now the youngest son Nagappan Pillai and his sister Padma remain.

With marriage, Rosy bade adieu to all her artistic inclinations and then onwards led the life of a housewife. It was a total transformation for her, including of her caste. By marrying an upper-caste man, a Nair, Rosy's Pulaya status was erased in her subsequent life. As hailing from a reputed Nair family in Nagercoil, Kesava Pillai and their son Nagappan Pillai could not afford to keep alive her former identity for fear of public humiliation. Some time in the early 1990s, Rosy died totally unsung. In 1997 Kesava Pillai too departed.

Both children are unable to provide any information regarding their mother's past life as Rosy. Nagappan Pillai, a retired bank officer, leads a happy domestic life in Nagercoil; Padma's life, with her husband and children in Madurai, has been much more unfortunate—in terms of both health and money.

Varied severe diseases, abject poverty, the untimely demise of one of her two sons and the mental instability caused by that death make the life of Padma wretched. She lives in a single room dwelling with her husband—who earns only a pitiable income—their widowed daughter and her baby. In a way, the tragedy of the Lost Heroine continues through Rosy's daughter Padma.

J.C. Daniel

During the rest of his life, J.C. Daniel did not make any other film. Daniel had always nurtured dreams of making films, and though by practising dentistry he could lead a comfortable life (and the rarity of owning a car in those days) later on he was in total financial ruin. According to known information, it was by investing in some dubious Tamil film ventures and trusting some friends that Daniel plunged into this plight. At any rate, during his twilight years Daniel, along with Janet, led a life of penury and suffering through diseases at Agastheeswaram, his birthplace.

As long as he was alive, Malayalam cinema did not recognize its creator. In 1975 Daniel died, followed by Janet in 1993. Since then, the memory of Daniel is shining brightly through the Lifetime Achievement Award for film personnel in Malayalam cinema instituted in his name by the Kerala government.

Among Daniel's five children, the only ones still living are Haris and Lalitha. Haris, who was an insurance company officer, lives in Salem; Lalitha, a housewife, lives in Thiruvananthapuram.